DMV Seminar
Band 12

Birkhäuser Verlag
Basel · Boston · Berlin

Jacobus H. van Lint, *1982-*
Gerard van der Geer

Introduction to Coding Theory and Algebraic Geometry

1988

Birkhäuser Verlag
Basel · Boston · Berlin

Authors

G. van der Geer
Mathematisch Instituut
Universiteit van Amsterdam
Roetersstraat 15
NL-1018 WB Amsterdam

J.H. van Lint
Dept. of Mathematics and
Computing Science
Eindhoven University of Technology
P.O. Box 513
NL-5600 MB Eindhoven

Library of Congress Cataloging in Publication Data

Lint, Jacobus Hendricus van, 1932 –
    Introduction to coding theory and algebraic geometry / Jacobus H.
van Lint, Gerard van der Geer.
        p.   cm. – – (DMV seminar ; Bd. 12)
    Includes index.
    ISBN 3–7643–2230–6
    1. Coding theroy.   2. Geometry, Algebraic.   I. Geer, Gerard van
der.   II. Title.   III. Series.
QA268.L573   1988   629.8'312 – – dc 19   88–19425

CIP-Titelaufnahme der Deutschen Bibliothek

Lint, Jacobus H. van:
Introduction to coding theory and algebraic geometry / Jacobus
H. van Lint ; Gerard van der Geer. – Basel ; Boston ; Berlin :
Birkhäuser, 1988
    (DMV-Seminar ; Bd. 12)
    ISBN 3–7643–2230–6
NE: Geer, Gerard van der:; Deutsche Mathematiker-Vereinigung:
    DMV-Seminar

© 1988 Birkhäuser Verlag, Basel
Printed in Germany
ISBN 3-7643-2230-6
ISBN 0-8176-2230-6

Contents

Preface 7

Part I: Coding Theory
          by Jacobus H. van Lint

1. Finite fields 11
2. Error-correcting codes 13
3. Linear codes 15
4. Cyclic codes 17
5. Classical Goppa codes 22
6. Bounds on codes 25
7. Self-dual codes 28
8. Codes from curves 30
   References 33

Part II: Algebraic Geometry
          by Gerard van der Geer

   Introduction 36
 I. Elementary concepts from algebraic geometry 37
 II. Divisors on algebraic curves 45
III. Goppa Codes 55
IV. Couting points on curves over finite fields 66
 V. Shimura curves and codes 73

   Index 82
   Index of notations 83

Preface

These notes are based on lectures given in the seminar on "Coding Theory and Algebraic Geometry" held at Schloss Mickeln, Düsseldorf, November 16–21, 1987.

In 1982 Tsfasman, Vladut and Zink, using algebraic geometry and ideas of Goppa, constructed a seqeunce of codes that exceed the Gilbert-Varshamov bound. The result was considered sensational. Furthermore, it was surprising to see these unrelated areas of mathematics collaborating.

The aim of this course is to give an introduction to coding theory and to sketch the ideas of algebraic geometry that led to the new result. Finally, a number of applications of these methods of algebraic geometry to coding theory are given.

Since this is a new area, there are presently no references where one can find a more extensive treatment of all the material. However, both for algebraic geometry and for coding theory excellent textbooks are available. The combination of the two subjects can only be found in a number of survey papers. A book by C. Moreno with a complete treatment of this area is in preparation.

We hope that these notes will stimulate further research and collaboration of algebraic geometers and coding theorists.

G. van der Geer, J.H. van Lint

Introduction to Coding Theory and Algebraic Geometry

Part I -- Coding Theory

Jacobus H. van Lint

1. Finite fields

In this chapter we collect (without proof) the facts from the theory of finite fields that we shall need in this course.

For more details we refer to Lidl and Niederreiter (1983), van Lint (1982), Mac Williams and Sloane (1977), Mc Eliece (1987).

A finite field with q elements is denoted by $\mathbb{F}_q$. (The notation is justified by the fact that two fields with q elements are isomorphic.) The notation $GF(q)$ is also used (Galois field). The easiest examples are the fields with p elements, where p is a prime number.

(1.1) $\mathbb{Z}/p\mathbb{Z}$ is a field if and only if p is a prime number. The other finite fields are residue class rings of $\mathbb{F}_p[x]$.

We observe:

(1.2) If $\mathbb{F}$ is a field then $\mathbb{F}[x]$ is a principal ideal ring.

The principal ideal generated by the polynomial $g(x)$ is denoted by $(g(x))$.
We shall need the following result.

(1.3) If $\mathbb{F}$ is a field then the residue class ring $\mathbb{F}[x]/(x^n-1)$ is a principal ideal ring and every ideal is generated by a divisor of (x^n-1).

For the construction of finite fields other than $\mathbb{F}_p$, we need polynomials $g(x)$ in $\mathbb{F}_p[x]$ that are *irreducible*. By the method of inclusion and exclusion one can show that if I_r denotes the number of monic irreducible polynomials of degree r in $\mathbb{F}_q[x]$, then

(1.4) $$\sum_{r\mid n} r\, I_r = q^n.$$

This shows that I_r is positive for all r.

(1.5) If p is prime and $g(x)$ is irreducible of degree r in $\mathbb{F}_p[x]$, then the residue class ring $\mathbb{F}_p[x]/(g(x))$ is a field with p^r elements.

It is an easy exercise to show that if $\mathbb{F}_q$ is a finite field, then q is a power of a prime p and $\mathbb{F}_p$ is a subfield. The number p is called the *characteristic* of the field.

Furthermore $(\mathbb{F}_q, +)$ is isomorphic to $(\mathbb{F}_p)^r$, where $q = p^r$. The multiplicative structure of $\mathbb{F}_q$ is also quite easy:

(1.6) The group $(\mathbb{F}_q \setminus \{0\}, \cdot)$ is cyclic. A generator of this group is called a *primitive* element of the field.

This shows that the elements of $\mathbb{F}_q$ form the set of all solutions of the equation $x^q - x = 0$ (in the closure of $\mathbb{F}_p$, where $q = p^r$). This fact combined with (1.4) easily leads to the theorem that up to isomorphism there is only one field with q elements ($q = p^r$, p *prime*). However, for some applications in coding theory, the particular representation of the field can make a difference! (cf. Mac Williams and Sloane 1977, Ch. 10 § 5). Furthermore, an easy consequence of (1.6) is:

12

(1.7) $I\!F_{p^r}$ is a subfield of $I\!F_{p^s}$ if and only if r divides s.

A fact, sometimes referred to as the "freshman's dream" is the equation $(a+b)^p = a^p + b^p$ if a and b are elements in a field of characteristic p. A consequence of this fact is $a(x^q) = (a(x))^q$ if $a(x) \in I\!F_q[x]$. This leads to a result that we use quite often:

(1.8) If $0 \neq f(x) \in I\!F_q[x]$ and if $f(\alpha) = 0$, where $\alpha \in I\!F_{q^s}$, then $f(\alpha^q) = 0$.

The converse is also true:

(1.9) If $f(x) \in I\!F_{q^s}[x]$ is monic and has the property that $f(\alpha^q) = 0$ for every α for which $f(\alpha) = 0$, then $f(x) \in I\!F_q[x]$.

Let $q = p^r$ and let β be an element of $I\!F_q$. The *minimal polynomial* $m(x)$ of β is the monic irreducible polynomial in $I\!F_p[x]$ for which $m(\beta) = 0$. By (1.8) and (1.9) we have

$$m(x) = (x-\beta)(x-\beta^p)(x-\beta^{p^2}) \cdots (x-\beta^{p^{s-1}}),$$

where s is the smallest positive integer such that $\beta^{p^s} = \beta$.

(1.10) Example. Let α be a primitive element of $I\!F_{2^4}$. Denote the minimal polynomial of α^i by $m_i(x)$. Then

$$x^{15} - 1 = (x-1)\, m_1(x)\, m_3(x)\, m_5(x)\, m_7(x),$$

where e.g. $m_7(x) = (x-\alpha^7)(x-\alpha^{14})(x-\alpha^{13})(x-\alpha^{11})$.

Note that $m_5(x) = x^2 + x + 1$, the unique irreducible polynomial of degree 2 in $I\!F_2[x]$. Since α^3 is a fifth root of unity we must have $m_3(x) = x^4 + x^3 + x^2 + x + 1$. The other two factors are $x^4 + x + 1$ and $x^4 + x^3 + 1$. Usually one chooses α such that the first of these is $m_1(x)$.

There are two more well known results about polynomials over $I\!F_q$ that we shall use:

(1.11) If $f(x) \in I\!F_q[x]$ and α is a zero of $f(x)$ in some extension field of $I\!F_q$, then α is a multiple zero if and only if it is also a zero of $f'(x)$.

(1.12) If the polynomials $a(x)$ and $b(x)$ in $I\!F_q[x]$ have greatest common divisor 1, then there are polynomials $p(x)$ and $q(x)$ such that $a(x)p(x) + b(x)q(x) = 1$.

Finally, we mention the *trace* function $Tr: I\!F_q \to I\!F_p$. If $q = p^r$ then for $\xi \in I\!F_q$

$$Tr(\xi) := \xi + \xi^p + \xi^{p^2} + \cdots + \xi^{p^{r-1}}.$$

Note that by the freshman's dream this is a linear mapping. Since the function is not identically 0, it takes every value the same number of times.

2. Error-correcting codes

We shall not go into details concerning all the technical applications of error-correcting codes. These include satellite pictures, telephone messages via glass fibre using light, compact disc audio system. The idea is as follows. We consider "*information*" presented as a very long sequence of symbols from a finite set called the "*alphabet*". In this course the alphabet will be a finite field $\mathbb{F}_q$. In the sequence each symbol occurs with equal probability. This information is sent to a receiver over a so-called "noisy channel". In the model that we consider there is a fixed (small) probability p_e that a symbol, that is sent over the channel, is changed into one of the other symbols (again, all equally likely). Such an event is called a "*symbol-error*" and p_e is the symbol-error probability. As a result a fraction p_e of the transmitted symbols arrives incorrectly at the receiver end of the channel. The aim of coding theory is to lower the probability of error (considerably) at the expense of spending some of the transmission time or energy on *redundant* symbols. The idea is explained in one sentence as follows. When we read printed text we recognize a printing error in a word because in our vocabulary there is only one word that resembles (is "sufficiently close to") the printed word.

In *block coding* the message is split into parts of say k symbols. The "encoding" is an injective mapping from $\mathbb{F}_q^k$ to $\mathbb{F}_q^n$ (where $n > k$). In $\mathbb{F}_q^n$ we introduce so-called *Hamming-distance*:

$$(2.1) \qquad d(\mathbf{x}, \mathbf{y}) := |\{1 \leq i \leq n, x_i \neq y_i\}|.$$

We define the *minimum distance* of the *code C* (i.e. the image of $\mathbb{F}_q^k$) by

$$(2.2) \qquad d = \min\{d(\mathbf{x}, \mathbf{y}) \mid \mathbf{x} \in C, \mathbf{y} \in C, \mathbf{x} \neq \mathbf{y}\}.$$

If $d = 2e + 1$ then C is an e-error-correcting code because if a received word has distance $\leq e$ to some codeword, then it has distance $> e$ to all other codewords.

Note that the toll we pay for the possibility of correcting errors is that we have to send n symbols over the channel to convey k information symbols to the receiver. This is expressed by saying that the code C has *information rate* $R := k/n$. The general definition for any subset C of $\mathbb{F}_q^n$ is $R = n^{-1} \log_q |C|$.

We shall always assume that the receiver uses so-called "*maximum-likelihood decoding*", i.e. a received word is "decoded" into a codeword that is closest (where a choice is made if this is not unique). Subsequently, the inverse of the encoding map yields the original information.

It is fairly obvious that we can make the probability of error after decoding as small as we like if we are willing to transmit at very low information rate. The reason that coding theory is interesting is given by Shannon's famous *channel coding theorem*. To explain this, we need a number called the *capacity* of the channel. This number depends on p_e and the size of the alphabet (i.e. q in our case). It lies between 0 and 1. (If $q = 2$ the capacity is $1 + p_e \log p_e + (1 - p_e) \log(1 - p_e)$, where logarithms are to the base 2.)

The theorem states that for any $\varepsilon > 0$ and for any R less than the capacity there is a code with information rate at least R, for which the probability of incorrect decoding (of a received word) is less than ε. The reader should realize that we do not specify k or n but only restrict the value of k/n. The "good" code promised by the theorem will have very large *word length n*.

To describe the situation that we are interested in in this course, we need a few more definitions.

(2.3) C is an (n, M, d) code over $\mathbb{F}_q$ if C is a subset of $\mathbb{F}_q^n$ with minimum distance d and $|C| = M$.

(2.4) $A_q(n, d) := \max\{M \mid \text{there exists an } (n, M, d) \text{ code over } \mathbb{F}_q\}$.

A code that achieves the bound of (2.4) is called *optimal*. From Shannon's theorem we know that we should study long codes. However, if the channel has symbol-error probability p_e, then we should expect an average of $p_e n$ errors per received word. To correct these we need minimum distance more than $2p_e n$. So, if we increase n, then d should increase proportionally. We introduce the parameter $\delta := d/n$ and define

(2.5) $\alpha(\delta) := \limsup\limits_{n \to \infty} n^{-1} \log_q A_q(n, \delta n)$.

Note that this function tells us something about the information rate of long codes with $d/n = \delta$. In the section on bounds on codes (Section 6) we shall describe the *Gilbert-Varshamov* bound, a lower bound for $\alpha(\delta)$ proved in 1952/1957 that was not improved until 1982. The new bound is obtained using methods from algebraic geometry and it is the purpose of this course to explain these methods and to give the necessary background on coding theory.

3. Linear codes

From now on we shall only consider linear codes.

(3.1) *Definition.* A q-ary linear code or $[n, k]$ code is a k-dimensional linear subspace of $\mathbb{F}_q^n$.

If the code has minimum distance d we shall write $[n, k, d]$ code. The information rate of such a code is k/n.

A linear code C is often described by a so-called *generator matrix* G. This is a matrix that has as its rows k basis vectors of C; (note that elements of $\mathbb{F}_q^n$ are called vectors or words). If G is a generator matrix for C, then $C = \{a\,G \mid a \in \mathbb{F}_q^k\}$, so encoding is multiplication by G. Since we are only interested in error correction and this does not depend on the order of the symbols in a word, we shall call two codes *equivalent* if one is obtained from the other by some permutation of the coordinate positions. Then we can assume w.l.o.g. that C has a generator matrix in so-called standard form: $G = (I_k P)$, where P is a k by $n-k$ matrix. In this case the first k symbols of a codeword are sometimes called information symbols and the remaining symbols are *parity check symbols*. (This name is due to the (historically) first example: a simple parity check code used on paper tape for computers. Here $q = 2$, $k = 5$, $n = 6$ and every codeword has an even number of ones, i.e. P is a column of ones).

(3.2) *Definition.* The *weight* $w(\mathbf{x})$ of a word is the number of nonzero symbols of $\mathbf{x}$. The *minimum weight* of a code C is the minimum of $w(\mathbf{c})$ over all nonzero codewords $\mathbf{c}$.

Note that for a linear code the minimum distance is equal to the minimum weight.

(3.3) *Definition.* If C is an $[n, k]$ code then we define the *dual code*

$$C^\perp \text{ by}$$

$$C^\perp := \{\mathbf{y} \in \mathbb{F}_q^n \mid \forall_{\mathbf{x} \in C} \, [<\mathbf{x}, \mathbf{y}> = 0]\},$$

where $<\mathbf{x}, \mathbf{y}> := \sum_{i=1}^{n} x_i y_i$ is the usual inner product.

Clearly $C^\perp$ is an $[n, n-k]$ code. Of special interest are *self-dual* codes, i.e. codes C for which $C^\perp = C$ (see Section 7).

A generator matrix H for the code $C^\perp$ is called a *parity check matrix* for C. The code C is given by

(3.4) $\qquad C = \{\mathbf{x} \in \mathbb{F}_q^n \mid \mathbf{x}H^\top = \mathbf{0}\}.$

If $G = (I_k P)$ is in standard form, then $H = (-P^\top I_{n-k})$ is a parity check matrix (because $G H^\top = 0$). For the $[6,5]$ binary single parity check code mentioned above, the equation in (3.4) is $x_1 + x_2 + \cdots + x_6 = 0$, i.e. the equation checks the parity of the received word. Note that this code cannot correct errors but it does detect the occurrence of a single error.

We mention a decoding method that is sometimes used in practice. For high-rate codes it is not too bad. The method is known as *syndrome decoding*. For any $\mathbf{x} \in \mathbb{F}_q^n$ the syndrome is defined as $\mathbf{x}H^\top$. For codewords the syndrome is $\mathbf{0}$. A received vector $\mathbf{x}$ with errors in it can be written as $\mathbf{x} = \mathbf{c} + \mathbf{e}$, where $\mathbf{c}$ is the transmitted word and $\mathbf{e}$ is known as the *error-vector*. If we pick a certain error-vector $\mathbf{e}$ and add it to all the codewords, the result is a coset of C in $\mathbb{F}_q^n$ and all the words in this coset have the same syndrome, namely $\mathbf{e}H^\top$.

This means that any vector in a coset is a candidate for the error-vector of a word in the same coset. By maximum likelihood decoding we should choose this vector so that it has minimum weight.

Decoding now goes as follows. For each coset of C we pick a member of minimal weight (often this element is unique). This is called the *coset leader*. We make a list of these coset leaders and their syndromes. When $\mathbf{x}$ is received, the syndrome is calculated, the leader is found by table lookup and $\mathbf{x}$ is decoded by subtracting the leader from $\mathbf{x}$. If, for example, we use a good binary code C of length 63 with $R = \dfrac{51}{63} = 0,8$, then C has over 2.10^{15} codewords but decoding involves only a check of a list of 4096 syndromes. Since this code can be chosen so that it has $d = 5$ (see 4.7), there are 63 coset leaders of weight 1 and 1953 of weight 2. One could list only these and their syndromes and in those cases that the syndrome of the received word is not in the list, the conclusion could be that more than two errors occurred.

Remark: If we transmit information over a binary symmetric channel with bit-error probability $p_e = 0.01$ using this code (with rate 0.8) we achieve an accuracy (after decoding) corresponding to a bit-error probability $p_e = 0.0005$.

We give one more definition.

(3.5) *Definition*. If C is a q-ary code of length n, then the *extended* code $\overline{C}$ is defined by

$$\overline{C} := \{(c_1, c_2, \cdots, c_n, c_{n+1}) \mid (c_1, c_2, \cdots, c_n) \in C, \sum_{i=1}^{n+1} c_i = 0\}.$$

(The symbol $c_n + 1$ is called *overall* parity check. It is 0 if and only if $c_1 + c_2 + \cdots + c_n = 0$.)

The best known examples of single error-correcting codes are the following codes. Let $n := (q^k - 1)/(q - 1)$. Since any nonzero column vector of length k has $q - 1$ nonzero multiples, it is possible to make a k by n matrix H in which no column is $\mathbf{0}$ and for which no two columns are linearly dependent. This implies that if $\mathbf{x}H^\top = \mathbf{0}$, then $\mathbf{x}$ must have weight at least 3. Therefore H is the parity check matrix of a $[n, n-k, 3]$ code that is called a *Hamming* code.

4. Cyclic codes

We now consider linear codes with even more regularity.

(4.1) *Definition.* A linear code C is called *cyclic* if

$$\forall_{(c_0, c_1, \ldots, c_{n-1}) \in C} \, [\, (c_{n-1}, c_0, \cdots, c_{n-2}) \in C \,].$$

From now on we make the convention $(n, q) = 1$.

To describe cyclic codes algebraically we observe that $\mathbb{F}_q^n$ as vector space is isomorphic to $\mathbb{F}_q[x]/(x^n - 1)$, if we ignore the multiplication in this ring. We now identify the word $(a_0, a_1, \cdots, a_{n-1})$ with the corresponding polynomial $a_0 + a_1 x + \cdots + a_{n-1} x^{n-1}$. Observe that multiplication by x now is nothing but a cyclic shift of the word. Since a cyclic code is linear by definition, we have:

(4.2) *Theorem.* A linear code C in $\mathbb{F}_q^n$ is cyclic if and only if C is an *ideal* in $\mathbb{F}_q[x]/(x^n - 1)$.

By (1.3) a cyclic code is a principal ideal generated by a polynomial $g(x)$, the *generator polynomial*, that divides $x^n - 1$. If $x^n - 1 = f_1(x) f_2(x) \cdots f_r(x)$ is the decomposition of $x^n - 1$ into irreducible factors we have 2^r choices for $g(x)$. (Some of these codes can be equivalent.)

The code M_i^- with generator $(x^n - 1)/f_i(x)$ is called an *irreducible* cyclic code. Every cyclic code is a direct sum of irreducible cyclic codes. (This is an example of a well known structure theorem for ideals in semisimple algebras). An irreducible cyclic $[n, k]$ code is isomorphic to $\mathbb{F}_q^k$.

Note that (1.11) and the convention $(n, q) = 1$ ensure that $x^n - 1$ has no multiple zeros. So the factors $f_i(x)$ are distinct.

Let $(x^n - 1) = g(x) h(x)$ in $\mathbb{F}_q[x]$. If $g(x) = g_0 + g_1 x + \cdots + g_{n-k} x^{n-k}$ and $h(x) = h_0 + h_1 x + \cdots + h_k x^k$, then

$$
G = \begin{bmatrix}
g_0 & g_1 & \cdots & g_{n-k} & 0 & 0 & \cdots & 0 \\
0 & g_0 & \cdots & & g_{n-k} & 0 & \cdots & 0 \\
 & & \ddots & & & \ddots & & \\
 & & & \ddots & & & \ddots & \\
0 & \cdots & \cdots & & g_0 & g_1 & \cdots & g_{n-k}
\end{bmatrix}
$$

is a generator matrix for the code C with generator polynomial $g(x)$ and one easily checks that

$$
H = \begin{bmatrix}
0 & 0 & \cdots & 0 & h_k & \cdots & h_0 \\
0 & \cdots & \cdots & h_k & & h_0 & 0 \\
 & & & & & & \\
h_k & & \cdots & h_0 & 0 & \cdots & 0
\end{bmatrix}
$$

is a parity check matrix for C. We call $h(x)$ the *check polynomial*. Observe that the code with $h(x)$ as generator polynomial is equivalent to $C^\perp$ (namely: obtained by reversing the order of the n symbols). So $C^\perp$ has generator polynomial $x^k h(x^{-1})$. C has dimension n-degree $g(x)$.

Let C be a cyclic code with generator $g(x) = f_1(x) \cdots f_t(x)$. Let β_i be a zero of $f_i(x)$, $1 \leq i \leq t$. By (1.8) and (1.9) we know all the zeros of $g(x)$. We remind the reader that if β_i lies in the extension field $\mathbb{F}_{q^m}$ of $\mathbb{F}_q$, then β_i can be interpreted as a column vector in $(\mathbb{F}_q)^m$. Now consider the t by n matrix over $\mathbb{F}_{q^m}$:

$$H := \begin{bmatrix} 1 & \beta_1 & \beta_1^2 & \cdots & \cdots & \beta_1^{n-1} \\ 1 & \beta_2 & \beta_2^2 & \cdots & \cdots & \beta_2^{n-1} \\ \vdots & \vdots & \vdots & & & \vdots \\ 1 & \beta_t & \beta_t^2 & \cdots & \cdots & \beta_t^{n-1} \end{bmatrix} .$$

This matrix can also be considered as a tm by n matrix over $\mathbb{F}_q$ (where we assume that all β_i are in $\mathbb{F}_{q^m}$). In a sense H is a parity check matrix for the code C. Indeed $\mathbf{c} = (c_0, c_1, \cdots, c_{n-1})$ is in C if and only if $c_0 + c_1 \beta_i + c_2 \beta_i^2 + \cdots + c_{n-1} \beta_i^{n-1} = 0$ for $1 \leq i \leq t$, because $\mathbf{c}$ is in C if and only if $c_0 + c_1 x + \cdots + c_{n-1} x^{n-1}$ is divisible by $g(x)$. If we interpret H as a matrix over $\mathbb{F}_q$, then it is possible that the rows are not linearly independent, i.e. a parity check matrix for C can be obtained from H by deleting rows if necessary.

(4.3) *Example.* Let $n := 2^m - 1$ and let β be a primitive element of the field $\mathbb{F}_{2^m}$. The cyclic code C defined by $C := \{c(x) \mid c(\beta) = 0\}$ has the (binary) m by n parity check matrix $H = (1 \; \beta \; \beta^2 \; \cdots \; \beta^{n-1})$. Since all the columns of H are different and nonzero, this code is the (binary) $[n, n-m]$ Hamming code defined in Section 3.

We now come to a generalization of Hamming codes, the so-called *BCH* codes (discovered by Bose, Ray Chaudhuri and Hocquenghem).

(4.4) *Definition.* Let β be a primitive n^{th} root of unity in an extension field of $\mathbb{F}_q$. Let $g(x)$ be the least common multiple of the minimal polynomials of $\beta^l, \beta^{l+1}, \cdots, \beta^{l+t-2}$. The cyclic code of length n over $\mathbb{F}_q$ with generator $g(x)$ is called a *BCH code* with *designed distance t*.

From now on we restrict ourselves to $l = 1$ (narrow-sense *BCH* codes). If $n = q^m - 1$, i.e. β is primitive in $\mathbb{F}_{q^m}$, the code is called a *primitive BCH* code.

(4.5) *Theorem.* The minimum distance of a *BCH* code with designed distance t is at least t. (This is called the *BCH bound*.)

Proof: As we saw earlier, a word $\mathbf{c} = (c_0, c_1, \cdots, c_{n-1})$ is in the code if and only if it has inner product 0 with every row of the matrix

(4.6) $$H := \begin{bmatrix} 1 & \beta & \beta^2 & \cdots & \beta^{n-1} \\ 1 & \beta^2 & \beta^4 & \cdots & \beta^{2(n-1)} \\ \vdots & & & & \vdots \\ 1 & \beta^{t-1} & \beta^{2(t-1)} & \cdots & \beta^{(n-1)(t-1)} \end{bmatrix} .$$

Any $t - 1$ columns of H form a Vandermonde matrix. Since this matrix has determinant $\neq 0$, the columns are linearly independent. It follows that $\mathbf{c}$ cannot have weight less than t. ∎

(4.7) *Example.* Let $q = 2$, $n = 63$, β a primitive element of $\mathbb{F}_{2^6}$. We take $g(x) = m_1(x)\, m_3(x)$. By (1.8) $g(x)$ has as zeros β^i, where $i = 1, 2, 4, 8, 16, 32$ or $i = 3, 6, 12, 24, 48, 33$. Since we have four consecutive powers of β among the zeros, the code with generator $g(x)$ has minimum distance at least 5 (in fact it is 5). So, this yields a $[63, 51, 5]$ binary code. (This code was used as an example in Section 3.)

A special case of *BCH* codes is obtained if we take $n = q - 1$.

(4.8) *Definition.* A *Reed-Solomon* code (*RS* code) is a primitive *BCH* code of length $n = q - 1$ over $\mathbb{F}_q$.

The generator of an *RS* code has the form $g(x) = \prod\limits_{i=1}^{d-1} (x - \alpha^i)$, where α is primitive in $\mathbb{F}_q$.

By (4.5) this code has minimum distance at least d and by the Singleton bound (6.7) the distance cannot be larger. Therefore *RS* codes are *MDS* codes (also see Section 6), i.e. $[n, n-d+1, d]$ codes.

Sometimes one considers the extended code of length $q = n + 1$. A codeword that gets an overall parity check $c_{n+1} = 0$ has $x = 1$ as a zero, so by (4.5) it has weight at least $d + 1$. It follows that the extended code has minimum distance $d + 1$, i.e. it is also *MDS*. We remark that *RS* codes are used in the compact disc error correcting code.

The original approach of Reed and Solomon was different. We take $n = q$. Number the elements of $\mathbb{F}_q$ as $\alpha_i := \alpha^i (0 \le i \le q-2)$, $\alpha_{q-1} = 0$, where α is primitive.

Let L be a set of polynomials of degree $< k$ in $\mathbb{F}_q[x]$. We define a code C by

$$C := \{(f(\alpha_0), f(\alpha_1), \cdots, f(\alpha_{q-1})) \mid f \in L\}.$$

Since a polynomial cannot have more than $k - 1$ zeros if its degree is less than k, the minimum weight (and hence the minimum distance) of C is at least $n - k + 1$. Since C has dimension k we see that C is an $[n, k, n-k+1]$ code, i.e. *MDS*. It is not difficult to see that this code is equivalent to an extended *RS* code as follows.

Let $f(x) = \sum\limits_{j=0}^{k-1} a_j x^j$ and write $c_i := f(\alpha_i)$, $0 \le i \le q - 2$.

Then if $1 \le l \le q - k - 1$ we have

$$\sum_{i=0}^{q-2} c_i (\alpha^l)^i = \sum_{j=0}^{k-1} a_j \sum_{i=0}^{q-2} (\alpha^{l+j})^i = 0,$$

since the inner sum is 0 because $1 \le l + j \le q - 2$. So, by (4.8) $\mathbf{c}$ is in the *RS* code with distance $q - k$.

As a preparation for the codes obtained from algebraic geometry we reformulate the second definition of *RS* codes. Let $\mathbb{P}$ be the projective line over $\mathbb{F}_q$. Let Q be the point $(1,0)$. We consider the space $\mathbb{L}$ of rational functions defined on $\mathbb{P}$ that do not have poles, even if we consider $\mathbb{P}$ over the closure of $\mathbb{F}_q$, except possibly in Q and then with order less than k. Let $P_0, P_1, \cdots, P_{n-1}$ be the points of $\mathbb{P}$ different from Q. Then the code defined above is the set $\{(f(P_0), f(P_1), \cdots, f(P_{n-1})) \mid f \in \mathbb{L}\}$ because the functions in $\mathbb{L}$ clearly have the form $f(x, y) = \dfrac{a(x,y)}{y^l}$, where $a(x, y)$ is a homogeneous polynomial of degree l, where $l < k$. The points P_i are $P_i = (\alpha^i, 1)$, $0 \le i \le n - 2$, $P_{n-1} = (0, 1)$.

We now generalize the idea of these codes a little more. We consider as alphabet $I\!F_{q^m}$ and take n distinct elements from this field, say $\alpha_1, \alpha_2, \cdots, \alpha_n$. Let $\mathbf{v} = (v_1, v_2, \cdots, v_n)$ be a vector of weight n over $I\!F_{q^m}$ and write $\mathbf{a} := (\alpha_1, \alpha_2, \cdots, \alpha_n)$.

(4.9) *Definition.* The *generalized Reed-Solomon* code $GRS_k(\mathbf{a}, \mathbf{v})$ has as codewords all $(v_1 f(\alpha_1), v_2 f(\alpha_2), \cdots, v_n f(\alpha_n))$, where f runs through the polynomials of degree $< k$ in $I\!F_{q^m}[x]$.

By the same arguments as used above, this code is *MDS*. From (4.8) we see that the dual of a Reed-Solomon code is again a Reed-Solomon code. It is not difficult to show that this is also true for generalized Reed-Solomon codes. (Hint: find a suitable basis for the polynomials of degree $< n - 1$).

We now return to *BCH* codes. We take the point of view of (2.5) and fix a value of δ. We consider a sequence of primitive *BCH* codes over some fixed field $I\!F_q$, with wordlength $n_i := q^{m_i} - 1$, where $m_i \to \infty$. We require each code to have minimum distance at least δn_i and denote the information rate of the code with length n_i by R_i. Now we are in for a disappointment! One can prove that $R_i \to 0$ for $i \to \infty$.

So we see that for a given channel (i.e. fixed symbol error probability) one cannot hope to find a good code by looking at long primitive *BCH* codes; (these codes are *bad*, cf. Mac Williams and Sloane (1977) § 9.5).

Luckily *BCH* codes (and hence *RS* codes) also have a nice property, namely that they are easy to decode. We describe an algorithm that is used to decode *BCH* codes. It is a modification due to Massey and others of an algorithm that was designed by Berlekamp. Consider a *BCH* code of length n over $I\!F_q$ with zeros $\beta^1, \beta^2, \cdots, \beta^{2t}$, where β is a primitive n^{th} root of unity in $I\!F_{q^m}$. We use the following notation. A codeword $C(x)$ is transmitted and we receive $R(x) = R_0 + R_1 x + \cdots + R_{n-1} x^{n-1}$ and call $E(x) := R(x) - C(x) = E_0 + E_1 x + \cdots + E_{n-1} x^{n-1}$ the error-vector. The set $M := \{i \mid E_i \neq 0\}$ is the set of positions where an error has occurred and we assume that the number of errors $e := |M|$ is $\leq t$. Define

$\sigma(z) := \prod_{i \in M} (1 - \beta^i z)$, the so-called *error-locator* (because there is an error in position s if and only if $\sigma(\beta^{-s}) = 0$).

$\omega(z) := \sum_{i \in M} E_i \beta^i \prod_{j \in M \setminus \{i\}} (1 - \beta^j z)$, the *error-evaluator* (since $E_i = \omega(\beta^{-i}) / \sigma'(\beta^{-i})$).

Clearly $\sigma(z)$ is a polynomial of degree $e \leq t$ and $\omega(z)$ has degree less than e. If we know these polynomials, then we know M (by factoring $\sigma(z)$ or by substituting all possible values of z) and from $\omega(z)$ we can then find the values of the E_i by substituting $z = \beta^{-i}$. We now make a formal calculation.

$$\frac{\omega(z)}{\sigma(z)} = \sum_{i \in M} \frac{E_i \beta^i}{1 - \beta^i z} = \sum_{i \in M} E_i z^{-1} \sum_{l=1}^{\infty} (\beta^i z)^l =$$

$$= \sum_{l=1}^{\infty} z^{l-1} E(\beta^l).$$

The point of the algorithm is that the first $2t$ coefficients on the right-hand side are known, because $E(\beta^l) = R(\beta^l)$ for $1 \leq l \leq 2t$ by definition of the code. So, if we write $S(z) := \sum_{l=1}^{2t} R(\beta^l) z^{l-1}$, we now have to find the unknown polynomials $\sigma(z)$ and $\omega(z)$ about which we know that

(4.10) $\omega(z) \equiv \sigma(z) S(z) \pmod{z^{2t}}$.

We now perform Euclid's algorithm to calculate the g.c.d. of $S(z)$ and z^{2t}. This is a very efficient algorithm that involves easily performed calculations. One can show (cf. Mc Eliece 1977, § 8.5) that the first time that we find a remainder of degree less than t we are done. More precisely: the algorithm starts with $0 . z^{2t} + 1 . S(z) = S(z)$ and produces a sequence of equations

$$s_n(z) . z^{2t} + t_n(z) . S(z) = r_n(z) ,$$

where the degree of $r_n(z)$ decreases until the g.c.d. is reached. Clearly the pair $r_n(z)$, $t_n(z)$ satisfies the congruence (4.10). When for the first time $r_n(z)$ has degree $< t$, we have found the required pair up to a constant factor (which is determined by the fact that $\sigma(0) = 1$).

5. Classical Goppa codes

Let us recall that in (4.4) a *BCH* code was defined as the set of words $(c_0, c_1, \cdots, c_{n-1}) \in \mathbb{F}_q^n$ such that $c_0 + c_1(\beta^j) + c_2(\beta^j)^2 + \cdots + c_{n-1}(\beta^j)^{n-1} = 0$ where β is a primitive n^{th} root of unity and $1 \le j < d$. Here d is the designed distance. We can rewrite this as follows:

$$(z^n - 1) \sum_{i=0}^{n-1} \frac{c_i}{z - \beta^{-i}} = \sum_{i=0}^{n-1} c_i \sum_{k=0}^{n-1} z^k (\beta^{-i})^{n-1-k} =$$

$$= \sum_{k=0}^{n-1} z^k \sum_{i=0}^{n-1} c_i (\beta^{k+1})^i = z^{d-1} p(z),$$

i.e.

(5.1) $$\sum_{i=0}^{n-1} \frac{c_i}{z - \beta^{-i}} = \frac{z^{d-1} p(z)}{z^n - 1},$$

for some polynomial $p(z)$ and vice versa, i.e. $(c_0, c_1, \cdots, c_{n-1})$ is in the code if and only if the left-hand side of (5.1) written as a rational function $a(z)/b(z)$ has a numerator divisible by z^{d-1}. We now generalize this as follows.

(5.2) *Definition*: Let $g(z)$ be a monic polynomial over $\mathbb{F}_{q^m}$ and let $L := \{\gamma_0, \gamma_1, \cdots, \gamma_{n-1}\} \subseteq \mathbb{F}_{q^m}$ (here $n = |L|$). We require that $g(\gamma_i) \ne 0$, $0 \le i < n$. The *Goppa code* $\Gamma(L, g)$ with Goppa polynomial $g(z)$ is the set of words $(c_0, c_1, \cdots, c_{n-1})$ in $\mathbb{F}_q^n$ for which

(5.3) $$\sum_{i=0}^{n-1} \frac{c_i}{z - \gamma_i} \equiv 0 \pmod{g(z)}.$$

Here (5.3) means that the numerator of the left-hand side, written as $a(z)/b(z)$, is divisible by $g(z)$. We can also make the convention that

(5.4) $$\frac{1}{z - \gamma} := \frac{-1}{g(\gamma)} \left[\frac{g(z) - g(\gamma)}{z - \gamma} \right], \text{ where the right-hand side is the unique polynomial}$$

$f(z) \bmod g(z)$ such that $(z - \gamma) f(z) \equiv 1 \pmod{g(z)}$.

From our introduction and (5.1) we see that if we take $g(z) = z^{d-1}$ and $L := \{\beta^{-i} \mid 0 \le i \le n - 1\}$, where β is a primitive n^{th} root of unity, then the Goppa code $\Gamma(L, g)$ is the narrow sense *BCH* code of designed distance d. We remark that not all *BCH* codes are also Goppa codes.

We can also interpret (5.2) as follows. Consider the vector space of rational functions $f(z)$ with the following properties:

i) $f(z)$ has zeros in all the points where $g(z)$ has zeros, with at least the same multiplicity;

ii) $f(z)$ has no poles, except possibly in the points $\gamma_0, \gamma_1, \cdots, \gamma_{n-1}$ and then of order 1.

Consider the code over $\mathbb{F}_{q^m}$ consisting of all the words $(\text{Res}_{\gamma_0} f, \text{Res}_{\gamma_1} f, \cdots, \text{Res}_{\gamma_{n-1}} f)$.

The Goppa code $\Gamma(L, g)$ is the "subfield subcode" consisting of all the words in the code with all coordinates in $\mathbb{F}_q$.

We shall now find a parity check matrix for $\Gamma(L, g)$. Let $g(z) = \sum_{i=0}^{t} g_i z^i$. Then

$\frac{g(z) - g(x)}{z - x} = \sum_{k+j \leq t-1} g_{k+j+1} x^j z^k$, so we have an easy expression for the polynomials on the right-hand side of (5.4). By (5.3) we must have, with $h_j := 1/g(\gamma_j)$,

$$\sum_{i=0}^{n-1} c_i h_i \sum_{k+j \leq t-1} g_{k+j+1} (\gamma_i)^j z^k = 0,$$

i.e. the coefficient of z^k is 0 for $0 \leq k \leq t - 1$. We see that $\mathbf{c}$ must have inner product 0 with the rows of the following matrix.

$$\begin{bmatrix} h_0 g_t & h_1 g_t & \cdots & h_{n-1} g_t \\ h_0(g_{t-1} + g_t \gamma_0) & h_1(g_{t-1} + g_t \gamma_1) & \cdots & h_{n-1}(g_{t-1} + g_t \gamma_{n-1}) \\ \vdots & & & \vdots \\ h_0(g_1 + g_2 \gamma_0 + \cdots + g_t \gamma_0^{t-1}) & \cdots & & h_{n-1}(g_1 + g_2 \gamma_{n-1} + \cdots + g_t \gamma_{n-1}^{t-1}) \end{bmatrix} .$$

Using elementary row operations we then find the following simple parity check matrix for $\Gamma(L, g)$:

$$H = \begin{bmatrix} h_0 & h_1 & \cdots & h_{n-1} \\ h_0 \gamma_0 & h_1 \gamma_1 & \cdots & h_{n-1} \gamma_{n-1} \\ \vdots & \vdots & & \vdots \\ h_0 \gamma_0^{t-1} & h_1 \gamma_1^{t-1} & & h_{n-1} \gamma_{n-1}^{t-1} \end{bmatrix} . \tag{5.5}$$

Note that if in (4.9) we take $\mathbf{v} := (h_0, h_1, \cdots, h_{n-1})$ and $\mathbf{a} := (\gamma_0, \gamma_1, \cdots, \gamma_{n-1})$, $k = t$, then the code $GRS_k(\mathbf{a}, \mathbf{v})$ has the matrix H of (5.5) as generator matrix. It follows that $\Gamma(L, g)$ is a subfield subcode of the dual of a certain Generalized Reed Solomon code, i.e. $\Gamma(L, g)$ is a subfield subcode of a Generalized Reed Solomon code!

Observe that in (5.5) we can again interpret each row as a set of m rows over $\mathbb{F}_q$. So we find (using (4.9)):

(5.6) *Theorem.* The Goppa code $\Gamma(L, g)$ has dimension $\geq n - mt$ and minimum distance $\geq t + 1$.

The fact that the minimum distance is at least $t + 1$ follows directly from the definition (5.3). Since the code is linear, we can consider the weight of $\mathbf{c}$. If this is w then the degree of the numerator $a(z)$ of the left-hand side of (5.3) is $w - 1$ (in fact less if $\sum_{i=0}^{n-1} c_i = 0$). So $w - 1$ is at least t. If $q = 2$ we can say a lot more.

Define $f(z) := \prod_{i=0}^{n-1} (z - \gamma_i)^{c_i}$. Then $\sum_{i=0}^{n-1} \frac{c_i}{z - \gamma_i} = f'(z) / f(z)$.

Since all exponents in $f'(z)$ are even, this is a perfect square. If we assume that $g(z)$ has no multiple zeros, then the fact that $g(z)$ divides $f'(z)$ implies that $g^2(z)$ divides $f'(z)$.

(5.7) *Theorem.* If $g(z)$ has no multiple zeros, then the binary Goppa code $\Gamma(L, g)$ has minimum distance at least $2t + 1$ (where $t := \text{degree } g(z)$).

We shall now show that the set of Goppa codes is a lot nicer than the *BCH* codes by showing that there are good long Goppa codes. (To appreciate what we mean by "good" the reader should first study Section 6.) We choose $n = q^m$, t, d and take $L = \mathbb{F}_{q^m}$. It remains to pick a Goppa polynomial $g(z)$ of degree t over $\mathbb{F}_{q^m}$ that is irreducible and such that $\Gamma(L, g)$ has minimum distance at least d. Suppose $c = (c_0, c_1, \cdots, c_{n-1})$ is a word of weight $j < d$, i.e. a word that we do not allow in the code. As we saw before, the numerator of $\sum_{i=0}^{n-1} \frac{c_i}{z - \gamma_i}$ has degree $j - 1$ and hence at most $\lfloor \frac{j-1}{t} \rfloor$ different polynomials of degree t can divide this numerator. Therefore we have to exclude at most $\sum_{j=1}^{d-1} \binom{n}{j} (q-1)^j \lfloor \frac{j-1}{t} \rfloor$ irreducible polynomials of degree t. This number is less than $\frac{d}{t} V_q(n, d)$ where (as in (6.1)) we use the notation $V_q(n, d) := \sum_{i=0}^{d} \binom{n}{i} (q-1)^i$. It is known that $\lim_{n \to \infty} n^{-1} \log_q V_q(n, \lfloor \delta n \rfloor) = H_q(\delta)$, where H_q is the entropy function (cf. (6.3)). A sufficient condition for the existence of the code we are looking for is that $\frac{d}{t} V_q(n, d)$ is less than the total number of irreducible polynomials of degree t over $\mathbb{F}_{q^m}$, which is known to be $\frac{1}{t} q^{mt} (1 + o(1))$. (In fact this follows from (1.4).) So, we find as a sufficient condition (after taking logarithms, $d = \lfloor \delta n \rfloor$, $n \to \infty$):

$$H_q(\delta) + o(1) < \frac{mt}{n} + o(1), \quad (m \to \infty).$$

From (5.6) we know that the codes we are considering have rate $\geq 1 - \frac{mt}{n}$. So we have proved the following theorem.

(5.8) *Theorem.* There exists a sequence of Goppa codes over $\mathbb{F}_q$ that have information rate tending to $1 - H_q(\delta)$, i.e. the rate tends to the Gilbert-Varshamov bound.

We remark that the decoding method that we discussed for *BCH* codes in Section 4 can be generalized to also decode Goppa codes. As in Section 4 we call the received word $R = C + E$. Using a similar notation we define

$$S(z) := \sum_{i=0}^{n-1} \frac{E_i}{z - \gamma_i} \quad \text{(using the convention of (5.4))}.$$

By (5.3) we can calculate $S(z)$ from R. Now we again define an error locator and error evaluator by

$$\sigma(z) := \prod_{i \in M} (z - \gamma_i), \quad \omega(z) := \sum_{i \in M} E_i \prod_{j \in M \setminus \{i\}} (z - \gamma_i).$$

Then clearly

$$S(z)\,\sigma(z) \equiv \omega(z) \quad (mod\ g(z))$$

and we are again in the situation of (4.10).

6. Bounds on codes

We now return to the problem of finding bounds on codes and the study of the function $\alpha(\delta)$ defined in (2.5). We need a few definitions and lemmas. If we consider the set of words in $\mathbb{F}_q^n$ that have distance at most d to a fixed word, then the cardinality of this set is

(6.1) $$V_q(n,d) := \sum_{i=0}^{d} \binom{n}{i} (q-1)^i.$$

We define the *entropy function* H_q on $[0, \frac{q-1}{q}]$ by

(6.2) $$H_q(0) := 0,$$
$$H_q(x) := x \log_q (q-1) - x \log_q x - (1-x) \log_q (1-x), \ 0 < x < \frac{q-1}{q}.$$

The following lemma can easily be proved using Stirling's formula (cf. van Lint 1982, 5.16):

(6.3) *Lemma.* For $0 \le \delta \le \frac{q-1}{q}$ we have

$$\lim_{n \to \infty} n^{-1} \log_q V_q(n, \lfloor \delta n \rfloor) = H_q(\delta).$$

Suppose C is a code of length n over $\mathbb{F}_q$ with minimum distance d and suppose that it is not possible to find a word not in C that has distance at least d to all codewords in C. Then clearly $|C| V_q(n, d-1) \ge q^n$. This simple argument is the proof of the Gilbert-Varshamov bound.

(6.4) *Theorem.* $A_q(n,d) \ge q^n / V_q(n, d-1)$.

If we take $d = \lfloor \delta n \rfloor$ and use (2.5) and (6.3), then we find the asymptotic Gilbert bound:

(6.5) *Theorem.* $\alpha(\delta) \ge 1 - H_q(\delta)$.

Suppose that we now consider only linear codes in $\mathbb{F}_q^n$. We claim that we find a result just as good as (6.4)!

(6.6) *Theorem:* If $q^n / V_q(n, d-1) > q^{k-1}$ then there exists an $[n, k, d]$ code over $\mathbb{F}_q$.

> Proof: For $k = 0$, the assertion is trivial. Suppose the inequality holds and that we have a $[n, k-1, d]$ code C_{k-1}. By the proof of (6.4) there is a word $\mathbf{x} \in \mathbb{F}_q^n$ that has distance at least d to all the words of C_{k-1}. If $a \in \mathbb{F}_q$ and $\mathbf{c} \in C_{k-1}$, then $w(a\mathbf{x}+\mathbf{c}) = w(\mathbf{x}+a^{-1}\mathbf{c}) = d(\mathbf{x}, -a^{-1}\mathbf{c}) \ge d$. Hence C_{k-1} and $\mathbf{x}$ span a linear code C_k with minimum distance d. □

As we already remarked in Section 2 the lower bound (6.5) was not improved until recently. The bound that we shall find from algebraic geometry (cf. alg. geom. 5.5) is

$$\alpha(\delta) + \delta \ge (\sqrt{q} - 1)^{-1}. \tag{*}$$

To see whether this improves (6.5) we first calculate the tangent to the curve (6.5) that has the same slope as (*). By differentiating (6.2) we find the equation

$$\log_q (q-1) - \log_q \delta + \log_q (1-\delta) = 1,$$

with solution $\delta_0 = (q-1)/(2q-1)$.

Therefore the line given by (*) intersects the curve (6.5)

if: $1 - H_q(\delta_0) < 1 - (\sqrt{q}-1)^{-1} - \delta_0$, i.e. $1 + (\sqrt{q}-1)^{-1} < \log_q(2q-1)$.

This is true for $q \geq 43$ but since in (*) q must be a square, the smallest value of q for which an improvement of (6.5) is found is $q = 49$.

It was pointed out by Manin (1982) that upper bounds for $A_q(n, \delta)$ could be used to prove theorems on algebraic curves as follows. The equation (*) is true for all q if we replace the right-hand side by $\gamma_q := \lim \inf g / n$ where we consider curves over $\mathbb{F}_q$ with n rational points ($n \to \infty$) and genus g. However, the line (*) must remain under the known upper bounds. At the time he wrote this, the bound for γ_2 could be improved using the best known upper bound for $A_2(n, \delta)$. At present the best known bounds for γ_q are better than what we can find using coding theory.

For the sake of completeness we now treat a number of upper bounds for $\alpha(\delta)$.

(6.7) *Theorem.* (Singleton bound.) $A_q(n, d) \leq q^{n-d+1}$.

    Proof: If C is a code with distance d, then deleting the last $d-1$ coordinates of each word in C yields a code of length $n - d + 1$ in which all the words are still different.   []

(6.8) *Corollary.* A $[n, k, d]$ code has $d \leq n - k + 1$.

Note that the proof of (6.7) implies that if equality holds in (6.8) then on any k positions the codewords take all possible q^k values (i.e. these k positions could be taken as "information positions"). Such a code is usually called a *maximum distance separable* code (*MDS* code). Note that if G is the generator matrix of such an *MDS* code, then any k columns of G are independent. This implies that the dual code has minimum distance at least $k + 1$. Therefore this distance is $k + 1$ (by (6.8)) and we see that the dual of an *MDS* code is again *MDS*.

One of the best known upper bounds is fairly obvious and asymptotically bad. This is the *sphere-packing bound*:

(6.9) *Theorem:* If $d = 2e + 1$ then $A_q(n, d) \leq q^n / V_q(n, e)$.

    Proof: The "spheres" of radius e around codewords are disjoint.   []

In order to prove a better bound we now consider a code C over $\mathbb{F}_q$ with M words of length n and distance d. We make a list of these words (as a matrix). We number the elements of $\mathbb{F}_q$ from 0 to $q - 1$. Consider column i of the matrix. Let the jth symbol of the alphabet occur m_j^i times in this column.

We calculate in two ways the sum of the distances of all ordered pairs of codewords. Taking all pairs of rows we find at least $M(M-1)d$. By looking at the columns we find (using Cauchy-Schwarz):

$$M(M-1)d \leq \sum_{i=1}^{n} \sum_{j=0}^{q-1} m_j^i (M - m_j^i) = \sum_{i=1}^{n} (M^2 - \sum_{j=0}^{q-1} (m_j^i)^2) \leq$$

$$\leq \sum_{i=1}^{n} (M^2 - q^{-1} (\sum_{j=0}^{q-1} m_j^i)^2) = n \frac{q-1}{q} M^2.$$

It follows that $M \le \dfrac{d}{d - n\frac{q-1}{q}}$ if $d > n \dfrac{q-1}{q}$.

This does not look very useful because we do not expect d to be so large. However we already have a result for $\alpha(\delta)$ from this inequality, namely

(6.10) $\alpha(\delta) = 0$ for $\dfrac{q-1}{q} \le \delta \le 1$.

To make use of the inequality for smaller values of δ we define the length n' by $n' := \lfloor \dfrac{q(d-1)}{q-1} \rfloor$; note that $n' < n$. We consider the last $n - n'$ symbols of all the codewords. There is a subset of M' codewords ending in the same $n - n'$ symbols, where $M' \ge q^{n'-n} M$.
For this subset the inequality derived above also holds, i.e.

$$q^{n'-n} M \le M' \le \frac{d}{d-n'\frac{q-1}{q}} \le d.$$

Taking $d = \delta n$, $n \to \infty$ we find the following theorem.

(6.10)*Theorem.* (Plotkin bound)

$$\alpha(\delta) \le 1 - \frac{q\,\delta}{q-1} \quad \text{for } 0 \le \delta \le \frac{q-1}{q} ,$$

$$\alpha(\delta) = 0 \quad \text{for } \frac{q-1}{q} \le \delta \le 1.$$

This leaves the shaded region in the following figure for possible values of $\alpha(\delta)$.

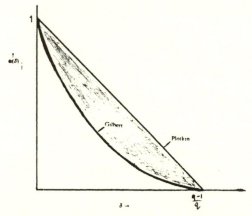

We remark that there are several sharper upper bounds than (6.10) (cf. Mac Williams and Sloane 1977).

7. Self-dual codes

A linear code C is called *self-dual* if $C = C^\perp$. Clearly the rate of such a code is ½. Many authors have studied such codes and discovered interesting connections with invariant theory and with lattice sphere packings (cf. Mac Williams and Sloane, 1977, Ch. 19). Recently there has been interest in geometric Goppa codes that are self-dual. For examples see alg.geom. § III. ref. [5], [6]. Here we give some theorems about self-dual codes.

A simple example of a self-dual code is the binary extended [8, 4, 4] Hamming code with generator matrix

$$G = \begin{bmatrix} 1 & 1 & 1 & 1 & 1 & 1 & 1 & 1 \\ 0 & 1 & 0 & 1 & 0 & 1 & 0 & 1 \\ 0 & 0 & 1 & 1 & 0 & 0 & 1 & 1 \\ 0 & 0 & 0 & 0 & 1 & 1 & 1 & 1 \end{bmatrix} .$$

As a second example we consider $q = 2^m$ and then construct the *RS* code C of length $n = q - 1$, dimension $k = \frac{1}{2} q$ and minimum distance $d = n - k + 1$ as in (4.8). The generator polynomial is $\prod_{i=1}^{\frac{1}{2} q - 1} (x - \alpha^i)$, where α is primitive in $\mathbb{F}_q$. As we saw in Section 4, the dual $C^\perp$ has generator polynomial $\prod_{i=0}^{\frac{1}{2} q - 1} (x - \alpha^i)$.

It follows that $C^\perp$ is the subcode of C consisting of all the words $(c_0, c_1, \cdots, c_{n-1})$ in C for which $c_0 + c_1 + \cdots + c_{n-1} = 0$. Therefore the extended code $\overline{C}$ is a $[q, \frac{1}{2} q, \frac{1}{2} q + 1]$ self-dual code. Since this is an *MDS* code we should consider it as a good code. It is natural to ask the question whether it is possible to find self-dual codes that are "good" in the asymptotic sense.

This means that, given the fact that we must have rate $= ½$, we should find out what can be said about d (or better $\delta = d/n$) if $n \to \infty$. The following theorems will provide us with an answer. (We consider only binary codes).

(7.1) *Theorem.* Let C be an $[n, k]$ binary code, where $n = 2t$, $1 \in C$, $C \subset C^\perp$. Then the number of $[n, t]$ self-dual codes that contain C is $\prod_{i=1}^{t-k} (2^i + 1)$.

Proof. For $k \leq m \leq t$ we shall count the number a_m of binary $[n, m]$ codes D such that $C \subseteq D \subseteq D^\perp$. Clearly $a_k = 1$. If D is such a code $(m < t)$ then $D^\perp$ is the union of 2^{n-2m} cosets of D. Since $1 \in C$, each of these cosets contains only vectors of even weight and hence the union of D with any other coset is a code D' of dimension $m + 1$ such that $C \subset D' \subset (D')^\perp$.

Exactly the same argument applied to C and D' shows that D' contains $2^{m+1-k} - 1$ subcodes of dimension m that also contain C.

Therefore $a_{m+1} = (2^{n-2m} - 1)/(2^{m-k+1} - 1) a_m$ $(k \leq m < t)$. $\quad\quad\quad\quad$ []

(7.2) *Corollary*:

a) There are $\prod_{i=1}^{\frac{1}{2}n-1} (2^i + 1)$ self-dual codes of length n (n even),

b) If $\mathbf{x}$ is a vector of even weight, $\mathbf{x} \notin \{\mathbf{0}, \mathbf{1}\}$, then there are $\prod_{i=1}^{\frac{1}{2}n-2} (2^i + 1)$ self-dual codes that contain

$\mathbf{x}$.

Proof: a) Every self-dual code contains $\{\mathbf{0}, \mathbf{1}\}$.

b) Apply (7.1) to the code C generated by $\mathbf{1}$ and $\mathbf{x}$.

[]

Now suppose n is even and $d = \delta n$. The number of even-weight vectors $\mathbf{x}$ with weight less than d is less than $V_2(n, d)$. Therefore (7.2) implies that a self-dual binary code of length n with minimum distance at least d exists if $V_2(n, d) < (2^{\frac{1}{2}n-1} + 1)$. From Lemma 6.3 we see that if $H_2(\delta) < \frac{1}{2}$, then a sequence of such codes with $n \to \infty$ exists. The Gilbert-Varshamov bound (6.5) states that for $H_2(\delta) = \frac{1}{2}$ we have $\alpha(\delta) \geq \frac{1}{2}$. We have proved:

(7.3) *Theorem*. There exists a sequence of binary self-dual codes that meets the Gilbert bound.

8. Codes from curves

We use the notation of alg. geom. § III.

1) *Reed-Solomon codes and BCH codes.*

Let β be a primitive n^{th} root of unity in $I\!F_{q^m}$ (m minimal).

We consider $I\!P^1 / I\!F_{q^m}$. Let $P_0 = (0,1), P_\infty = (1,0)$ and define the divisor $D := \sum_{j=1}^{n} P_j$, where $P_j := (\beta^j, 1)$, $1 \le j \le n$. We define the divisor G by $G := a P_0 + b P_\infty$, $a \ge 0$, $b \ge 0$. In this case $L(G)$ consists of the rational functions $\dfrac{b(x)}{a(x)}$ over $I\!F_{q^m}$ with degree $a(x) \le a$, degree $b(x) \le b$. It follows that $L(G)$ has dimension $a + b + 1$ and as basis the functions x^i ($-a \le i \le b$). A generator for the code $C(D, G)$ has as rows $(\beta^i \beta^{2i} \cdots \beta^{ni})$ where $-a \le i \le b$. If $(c_1, c_2, \cdots, c_n)$ is a codeword, then $\sum_{j=1}^{n} c_j (\beta^l)^j = 0$ if $a + 1 \le l \le n - b - 1$. Therefore the code is a Reed-Solomon code (in the sense of (4.9)). The subfield subcode found by restriction to $I\!F_q$ is a *BCH* code with designed distance $n - (a+b)$. This is the bound we also find for the distance of $C(D, G)$.

2) *Codes from Hermitean curves*

We consider the alphabet $I\!F_q$, where $q = r^2$ (r a power of p). Consider the so-called *hermitean curve X* in $I\!P^2$ over $I\!F_q$ given by

(8.1) $\qquad x^{r+1} + y^{r+1} + z^{r+1} = 0.$

By the Plücker formula (alg.geom. § II. 4) the curve X has genus $g = \dfrac{r(r-1)}{2}$, i.e. $g = \frac{1}{2}(q - \sqrt{q})$. As an exercise we actually calculate the number of rational points of X. If one of the coordinates is 0, we may take another to be 1 and then we have $r + 1$ solutions for the third coordinate, since $x^{r+1} = 1$ has $r + 1$ solutions in $I\!F_q$. So, there are $3(r+1)$ points with $xyz = 0$. If $xyz \ne 0$, we may take $z = 1$ and we can choose the value of y^{r+1} to be any element in $I\!F_r \setminus \{0, 1\}$. This again leaves us with $r + 1$ choices for x. In this way we find $(r-2)(r+1)^2$ solutions. The total number of rational points of X is therefore $1 + q \sqrt{q}$.

Now let Q be the point $(0, 1, 1)$ and define the divisors $G := mQ$, $D :=$ sum of all the other rational points. We take $q - \sqrt{q} < m < q \sqrt{q}$. We find the geometric Goppa code $C(D, G)$ with length $n = q \sqrt{q}$, dimension $k = m - g + 1$ and minimum distance $d \ge n - m = n - k - g + 1$.

Again as an exercise, we treat a very simple example. Take $q = 4$ an write $I\!F_4 = \{0, 1, \omega, \bar{\omega}\}$ where $\bar{\omega} = \omega^2 = \omega + 1$. In this case $g = 1$. If we take $m = 2$ then $C(D, G)$ has dimension 2. As basis we need two functions belonging to $L(2Q)$. Clearly $f(x, y, z) = 1$ is one of these. We claim that $x / (y + z)$ is another. This follows from the fact that on X

$$\frac{x}{y+z} = \frac{x(y^2 + yz + z^2)}{(y+z)(y^2 + yz + z^2)} = \frac{y^2 + yz + z^2}{x^2},$$

i.e. Q is indeed a pole of order 2 (x is a local parameter in Q).

Substituting the coordinates of the eight rational points $\neq Q$ we find a generator matrix with a row of ones and a second row with each of the elements $0, 1, \omega, \bar{\omega}$ two times. Obviously this code has distance 6 as the theorem promises. If we take $m = 3$, we must find one more basis function, now with a pole of order 3 in Q. We leave it as an exercise to find such a function and to check by hand that d is 5. If we then take $m = 4$ we can add the function $(x / (y+z))^2$ to our basis. The resulting code is an [8, 4, 4] code that is *self-dual*.

Now, let us use the code $C(D, G)$ of length $n = 64$ and rate ½ over $I\!\!F_{16}$ for comparison. We assume that we have a very poor channel with $p_e = 0.04$. We compare the code with a Reed-Solomon code over the same alphabet. Since this code has length 16 we shall consider four words of the second code as one message. The code $C(D, G)$ has $m = 37$ and $d = 27$. It is already far better than a *BCH* code over this alphabet (it has $d \leq 18$). The error probability for a word (of 64 letters from $I\!\!F_{16}$) for $C(D, G)$ is 2.10^{-7} as compared to 8.10^{-4} for the *RS* code.

We remark that it is easy to find a basis for $L(m Q)$, i.e. to find a generator matrix for the code. Consider the functions $f(x, y, z) = \dfrac{x^i y^j}{(y+z)^l}$, where $0 \leq i \leq 4$, $j \geq 0$, $i + j = l$. Using (8.1) with $r = 5$ we can replace $(y+z)^{-l}$ by $(y^4 + y^3 z + y^2 z^2 + y z^3 + z^4)^l x^{-5l}$. Therefore $f(x, y, z)$ has a pole of order $5l - i$ in Q. Clearly these functions are independent. For $5l - i \leq 37$ there are exactly 32 triples (i, j, l) satisfying the conditions.

3) *New bounds for binary codes.*

We consider an example that was considered before (cf. alg. geom. 1.9, 3.12)

Let X be the Klein quartic over $I\!\!F_8$ (genus $g = 3$):

$$(8.2) \qquad x^3 y + y^3 z + z^3 x = 0.$$

The points over $I\!\!F_8$ are easily found. Let α be a primitive element satisfying $\alpha^3 + \alpha + 1 = 0$. Clearly the three points $(0, 0, 1)$, $(0, 1, 0)$ and $(1, 0, 0)$ are on X. If $xyz \neq 0$ we take $z = 1$, $y = \alpha^i$ ($0 \leq i \leq 6$). Writing $x = \alpha^{3i} \xi$ we find $\xi^3 + \xi + 1 = 0$, i.e. $\xi \in \{\alpha^i, \alpha^2, \alpha^4\}$. So X has 24 points. Take $Q := (0, 0, 1)$, $G = 10Q$, D the sum of the 23 other points. Then the code $C := C(D, G)$ has length 23, distance 23 - *deg* $G = 13$, dimension $= 10 - g + 1 = 8$. Since $I\!\!F_8 \cong (I\!\!F_2)^3$ we can consider codewords in C as 3 by 23 matrices over $I\!\!F_2$. We now extend the code by adding a fourth row as "parity row" (making a 4 by 23 matrix over $I\!\!F_2$ with column of even weight). It is obvious that we have constructed a binary [92, 24, 26] code.

By leaving out one bit we find a binary [91, 24, 25] code. This example (due to Barg et al 1987) beats the best known code for $n = 91, d = 25$.

4) *A geometric MDS code* (example due to R. Pellikaan)

Consider the curve X with equation

(8.3) $\qquad x^2 y + \omega y^2 z + \bar{\omega} z^2 x = 0$

over $I\!F_4 := \{0, 1, \omega, \bar{\omega}\}$. The curve X has genus 1 and is nonsingular. The nine rational points of X are:

	P_1	P_2	P_3	P_4	P_5	P_6	Q_1	Q_2	Q_3
x	1	0	0	1	1	1	ω	1	1
y	0	1	0	ω	$\bar{\omega}$	1	1	ω	1
z	0	0	1	$\bar{\omega}$	ω	1	1	1	ω

The line $x + y + \bar{\omega} z = 0$ is tangent to X at Q_1 and also intersects X in Q_2. Let $G := 2 Q_1 + Q_2$ and $D := P_1 + \cdots + P_6$.

To describe the code $C(D, G)$ we use as basis for $L(G)$ the functions $x / (x + y + \bar{\omega} z)$, $y / (x + y + \bar{\omega} z)$ and $\bar{\omega} z / (x + y + \bar{\omega} z)$. This gives as generator matrix

$$\begin{bmatrix} 1 & 0 & 0 & 1 & \omega & \omega \\ 0 & 1 & 0 & \omega & 1 & \omega \\ 0 & 0 & 1 & \omega & \omega & 1 \end{bmatrix}$$.(Note that the code is equivalent to its dual).

Our bounds show that this [6, 3] code has $d \geq 3$ but in fact this is a [6, 3, 4] code, i.e. it is an *MDS* code. This contradicts an assertion of Driencourt and Michon (1986) that none of the [$q + 2, q - 1, 4$] codes is elliptic.

References

- A.M. Barg, S.L. Katsman and M.A. Tsfasman (1987), Algebraic Geometric Codes from Curves of Small Genus, Probl. of Information Transmission **23** (1987), 34-38.

- Y. Driencourt and J.F. Michon (1986), Rapport sur les Codes Géométriques, Univ. Aix-Marseille II et Université Paris 7.

- R. Lidl and H. Niederreiter (1983), Finite Fields, Addison-Wesley, Reading-Mass.

- J.H. van Lint (1982), Introduction to Coding Theory, Springer Verlag, New York.

- F.J. Mac Williams and N.J.A. Sloane (1977), The Theory of Error-Correcting Codes, North Holland, Amsterdam.

- Y.I. Manin (1982), What is the maximal number of points on a curve over F_2? J. Fac. Sci. Univ. Tokyo, Sec. Ia, 28, No 3, 715-720.

- R.J. Mc Eliece (1977), The Theory of Information and Coding, Encyclopedia of Math. and its Applic. Vol. 3, Addison-Wesley, Reading-Mass.

- R.J. Mc Eliece (1987), Finite Fields for Computer Scientists and Engineers, Kluwer, Boston.

Introduction to Coding Theory and Algebraic Geometry

Part II -- Algebraic Geometry

Gerard van der Geer

Introduction.

These notes are the slightly extended version of the notes of my DMV lectures on algebraic geometry and coding,to be more precise, the algebraic geometry counter part to the lectures of van Lint on coding. Since the audience was rather inhomogeneous it was necessary to start from scratch and explain or recall elementary notions from algebraic geometry. The aim of the lectures was to sketch the main ideas behind the recent succesful application of curves and in particular modular curves to coding theory. Although we review basic notions from algebraic geometry in the first two lectures this should not be seen as a substitute for a more thorough approach. If the reader really wants to apply algebraic geometry to coding he should make himself well-acquainted with the basic results. Good textbooks for this purpose are now available. We refer to the list of references at the end of Lecture 1 and Lecture 2.

After reviewing the necessary algebraic geometry in Lecture 1 and Lecture 2 we define the geometric Goppa codes in Lecture 3. We first treat the standard material and then we show how one can determine the actual minimum distance for geometric Goppa codes using the subtle geometry of divisors on a curve. In general the determination of this minimum distance is a very non-trivial problem. As a result we can give several examples of good Goppa codes obtained from higher genus curves, in particular from the Klein curve. In Lecture 4 we treat the zeta function of a curve over a finite field. In Lecture 5, the last lecture, we sketch the application of modular curves to Goppa codes. We hope to give the reader an idea how modular curves are used. Since the theory of modular curves is deep we cannot pretend to give more than a rough outline here.

I. Elementary concepts from algebraic geometry.

1. Let k be an algebraically closed field. We denote by A_k^n or simply by A^n the n-dimensional affine space over k. It carries a topology, the Zariski-topology whose closed sets are the sets of zeroes of ideals a of $k[x_1,...,x_n]$:

$$V(a) = \{(x_1,...,x_n) \in A^n : f(x_1,...,x_n) = 0 \text{ for all } f \in a \}.$$

A closed set B of a topological space is called irreducible if B cannot be written as the union of two proper closed subsets B_1 and B_2 of B. The set $V(a)$ is irreducible if and only if a is a prime ideal. By the Hilbert Nullstellensatz the points of A_k^n correspond 1-1 to the maximal ideals of $k[X_1,...,X_n]$: to a point $(x_1,...,x_n)$ we associate the ideal

$$\{ f \in k[X_1,...,X_n] : f(x_1,...,x_n) = 0\}$$

and to a maximal ideal its unique zero. This correspondence will enable us to translate geometry into algebra and vice versa.

An affine variety X in A_k^n is the set of zeroes of a prime ideal p of $k[X_1,...,X_n]$. It is provided with the induced topology. Its points correspond 1-1 to the maximal ideals of $k[X_1,...,X_n]$ which contain p, i.e. to the maximal ideals of

$$k[X] = k[X_1,...,X_n]/p.$$

This quotient ring is called the coordinate ring of X. It is a domain and a finitely generated k-algebra. Its field of quotients $k(X)$ is called the function field of X.

Let X in A_k^n and Y in A_k^m be two affine varieties. A map $\phi: X \rightarrow Y$ is called a morphism if there exist m polynomials $f_1,...,f_m$ in $k[X_1,...,X_n]$ such that ϕ is given by

$$\phi(x) = (f_1(x_1,...,x_n),...,f_m(x_1,...,x_n)) \qquad \text{for all } x \text{ in } X.$$

A morphism is a continuous map. Such a morphism induces a k-algebra homomorphism

$$\phi^* : k[Y] \rightarrow k[X] \qquad \text{as follows.}$$

If $g \in k[Y_1,...,Y_n]$ represents $g' \in k[Y]$ then define $\phi^*(g')$ as the class of $g(f_1,...,f_m)$. This is well-defined. Conversely, let $\psi : k[Y] \rightarrow k[X]$ be a k-algebra homomorphism and let f_i be the image under ψ of the class of Y_i. Representatives of the f_i define a morphism $\xi : X \rightarrow Y$. One checks $\xi^* = \psi$. A morphism $\phi: X \rightarrow Y$ is called an isomorphism if there exists a morphism $\psi: Y \rightarrow X$ with $\phi \cdot \psi = id_Y$ and $\psi \cdot \phi = id_X$. From what was just said one deduces immediately the following basic fact.

(1.1) Proposition. Two affine varieties X and Y (over k) are isomorphic if and only if $k[X]$ and $k[Y]$ are isomorphic as k-algebras.

Therefore all the information stored in an affine variety can be read off from its coordinate ring. A further consequence: if $\mathrm{Mor}(X,Y)$ denotes the set of morphisms of X to Y we have a bijection $\mathrm{Mor}(X,Y) \longleftrightarrow \mathrm{Hom}_k(k[Y],k[X])$. In particular, $\mathrm{Mor}(X,A^1) \longleftrightarrow \mathrm{Hom}_k(k[A^1],k[X]) \cong k[X]$. In this way the elements of $k[X]$ can be viewed as "functions".

The topology on X has a basis consisting of open sets of the form
$$D(f) = \{ x \in X : f(x) \neq 0 \}.$$
Then $D(f)$ is again an affine variety (it can be given in A^{n+1} by the equations of $X \subset A^n$ and the equation $X_{n+1}f = 1$) and the coordinate ring of such an open set is $k[X][1/f]$.

For example, if $X = \mathbb{P}^1$, then for $f \in k[X]$, $f \notin k$ the complement of the set $D(f)$ consists of finitely many points. So non-empty open sets are very big and two non-empty open sets have a non-zero intersection.

2. A polynomial $f \in k[X_0,...,X_n]$ is called homogeneous if $f(\lambda X_0,...,\lambda X_n) = \lambda^d f$ for some d (called the degree of f) and all $\lambda \neq 0$ in k. An ideal in $k[X_0,...,X_n]$ is called homogeneous if it is generated by homogeneous elements. Assume again that $\overline{k}$ is an algebraically closed field. A projective algebraic variety X is the set of zeroes in projective space $\mathbb{P}^n$ of a homogeneous prime ideal $\overline{p}$ of $\overline{k}[X_0,...,X_n]$. To it we can associate the homogeneous coordinate ring, but unfortunately this does not possess the nice properties that we have for affine varieties. An open subset of a projective algebraic variety is called a <u>quasi-projective variety</u>. If k is a field contained in $\overline{k}$ then we say that X is defined over k if $\overline{p}$ is generated by a prime ideal p of $k[X_0,...,X_n]$.

In the following we shall assume that $k = \overline{k}$ is algebraically closed. Let x be a point of an affine (resp. projective) variety X. Let U be an open neighbourhood of x. We say that a continuous map ϕ of U to A^1 is a regular function in x if there exist polynomials f,g in $X_1,...,X_n$ (resp. homogeneous polynomials of the same degree in $X_0,...,X_n$) such that $g(p) \neq 0$ and $\phi = f/g$ in an open neighbourhood of x. It is called regular on U if it is regular in all $x \in U$. The regular functions on U form a ring which is denoted $O_X(U)$ or $O(U)$.

Let x be a point of X. Consider pairs (U,f), where U is an open neighbourhood of x and f is a regular function on U. Define an equivalence relation:
$$(U,f) \approx (V,g) \quad \Leftrightarrow \quad f = g \text{ on } U \cap V.$$
The equivalence classes form a ring (by adding and multiplying values of functions). This ring is denoted O_x. It is called the <u>local ring</u> of x. It is a local ring in the algebraic sense that it has only one maximal ideal: the classes of those (U,f) where $f(p) = 0$. We view

elements of the local ring O_x as functions defined on some open neighbourhood of x. In case the variety is affine and m is the maximal ideal corresponding to x (by the Hilbert Nullstellensatz, see above) the local ring is the localization $k[X]_m$ of $k[X]$ at m , i.e. $\{a/b \in k(X) : b \notin m\}$. Using this one has for an affine variety

$$O(X) = \cap_x O_x = \cap_m k[X]_m \text{ inside the quotient field of } k[X]$$

and this intersection is $k[X]$ as an easy exercise in algebra shows.

Let X be a quasi-projective variety and consider pairs (U,f) with U non-empty and open in X and $f \in O(U)$. Define again an equivalence relation

$$(U,f) \approx (V,g) \quad \Leftrightarrow \quad f = g \text{ on } U \cap V.$$

The equivalence classes are called <u>rational functions</u> and form a field, called the <u>function field</u> $k(X)$ of X. In the case of an affine variety one finds again the field of quotients of $k[X]$. Obviously, if U is a non-empty subset of X then $k(U) = k(X)$.

Let X and Y be quasi-projective varieties. A continuous map f: $X \to Y$ is called a <u>morphism</u> if for every open U in Y and every $g \in O(U)$ the composition g·f is a regular function on $f^{-1}(U)$. For an affine variety morphisms in the earlier sense are certainly morphisms in this new sense. But a morphism in the new sense induces a k-algebra homomorphism on the coordinate rings, therefore it is a morphism in the old sense and the two concepts coincide there. We also consider pairs (U,f), where U is a non-empty open subset of X and f : $U \to Y$ is a morphism. The equivalence classes under the relation

$$(U,f) \approx (V,g) \quad \Leftrightarrow \quad f = g \text{ on } U \cap V$$

are called <u>rational maps</u> from X to Y. A rational map is called dominant if for some (and hence every) representative (U,f) the image f(U) lies dense. By composition of functions a dominant rational map from X to Y gives rise to a k-algebra homomorphism $k(Y) \to k(X)$ of the function fields . Conversely, given a k-algebra homomorphism $\phi: k(Y) \to k(X)$ we find a rational map as follows. Choose an open affine U in Y and choose generators u_i for $k[U]$. Let $v_i = \phi(u_i)$ and choose an affine open V such that the v_i are regular on V. The k-algebra homomorphism $k[U] \to k[V]$ given by $u_i \to v_i$ induces a morphism $V \to U$ which represents a rational map from X to Y. We call X and Y <u>birationally equivalent</u> if there exists a rational map r_1 from X to Y and a rational map r_2 from Y to X such that the compositions $r_1 \cdot r_2$ and $r_2 \cdot r_1$ are the identity on a non-empty open set of Y and X. We can deduce now:

(1.2) Proposition. X and Y are birationally equivalent if and only if their function fields are isomorphic as k-algebras.

(1.3) Example. Let $X=Y = \mathbb{P}^2$ and let $r_1 : X \to Y$ be given by $(x_0 : x_1 : x_2) \to$ $(x_0x_1 : x_0x_2 : x_1x_2)$ if at least two coordinates are non-zero. It is a birational map with inverse $r_2 : Y \to X$ which sends $(y_0 : y_1 : y_2)$ to $(y_0y_1 : y_0y_2 : y_1y_2)$ if at least two coordinates are non-zero.

(1.4) Example. The parametrization $\mathbb{A}^1 \to X = V(y^2 - x^3) \subseteq \mathbb{A}^2$ given by $t \to (t^2, t^3)$ is a birational map with inverse $(x,y) \to x/y$ if $y \neq 0$. It is not an isomorphism since $k[t]$ is not isomorphic to $k[x,y]/(x^3 - y^2)$.

Projective varieties have the following important property. If X is a projective variety and $\phi : X \to Y$ is a morphism then the image of ϕ is closed in Y. So if $\phi : X \to \mathbb{A}^1 \subset \mathbb{P}^1$ is a regular function on a projective variety X, then the image is closed in $\mathbb{A}^1$ and in $\mathbb{P}^1$ and irreducible, hence consists of one point. There are no regular functions other than constant functions on a projective variety. This shows the need for introducing concepts like rational functions and rational maps.

We define the <u>dimension</u> of X as the transcendence degree of the function field $k(X)$ of X. We denote it by $\dim(X)$. A variety of dimension 1 is called an <u>algebraic curve</u>. For example, an irreducible homogeneous polynomial $f \in k[x,y,z]$ of degree ≥ 1 defines an algebraic curve in $\mathbb{P}^2$.

A point x of a variety X is called a <u>non-singular point</u> if the $O_x/m_x (= k)$-module m_x/m_x^2 (i.e. k-vector space) has the same dimension as X.(In general $\dim_k m_x/m_x^2 \geq \dim(X)$.). The dual of this k-vector space m_x/m_x^2 is called the (Zariski-) tangent space. The set of non-singular points of X is a non-empty open subset of X. We call X <u>non-singular</u> or <u>smooth</u> if all its points are non-singular.

For a curve given in $\mathbb{P}^2$ by an equation $F = 0$, where $F \in k[X,Y,Z]$ is an irreducible polynomial, we have

$P = (x:y:z)$ is a singular point if and only if $F(P) = \frac{\partial F}{\partial X}(P) = \frac{\partial F}{\partial Y}(P) = \frac{\partial F}{\partial Z}(P) = 0$,

as we shall see shortly.

Recall the definition of a discrete valuation v on a field K. It is a homomorphism of the multiplicative group K^* of K onto $\mathbb{Z}$ such that $v(x+y) \geq \min(v(x),v(y))$. Such a discrete valuation defines a discrete valuation ring $R = \{ x \in K^* : v(x) \geq 0 \} \cup \{0\}$. We often put $v(0) = \infty$. The quotient field of R is K. A domain R is called a discrete valuation ring if there exists a discrete valuation v on its quotient field K such that $R = \{ x \in K^* : v(x) \geq 0 \} \cup \{0\}$.

(1.5) Lemma. Let X be an algebraic curve and x a point on X. Then x is non-singular if and only if the local ring O_x is a discrete valuation ring.

Proof. Suppose that x is a non-singular point . Let $f \in O_x$. We define $v(f) = n$ if $f \in m^n$, but $f \notin m^{n+1}$. If f/g is an element of k(X) then we set $v(f/g) = v(f) - v(g)$. This defines a discrete valuation on k(X). Conversely if O_x is a discrete valuation ring then m/m^2 has dimension one (it is generated by the class of an element t with $v(t) = 1$). ◊

An element t with $v(t) = 1$ is called a <u>local parameter</u> <u>(or local coordinate)</u>.

(1.6) Lemma. Let X be a non-singular curve and $f: X \to \mathbb{P}^n$ a rational map. Then f can be extended to a morphism.

Proof. Let $x \in X$ and let f be represented locally around x by $y \to (g_0(y):...:g_n(y))$. Multiply all g_i by the same power t^e of t such that $v(t^e g_i) \geq 0$ and $\min (v(t^e g_i)) = 1$. Then f can be represented locally as $y \to (t^e g_0(y):...:t^e g_n(y))$ which shows that f is well-defined there. ◊

(1.7) Corollary. Non-singular projective curves are classified by their function fields.

Proof. If X and Y are two non-singular projective curves and $f : X \to Y$ is a birational map, then it can be extended to an isomorphism. ◊

If X is a non-singular projective curve with function field k(X) we can read off all information about X from k(X). Indeed, we know that a point $x \in X$ gives rise to a discrete valuation of k(X), trivial on k. But conversely, every discrete valuation of k(X), trivial on k , determines a point of X, namely, the common zero of all f in k(X) with $v(f) \geq 1$. The above suggests to start with a function field K of transcendence degree 1 over k and attach a non-singular projective curve X to it with k(X) = K.

Thus after all, we might have started with a field K of algebraic functions of one variable over k. The field uniquely determines the isomorphism class of a smooth projective curve X defined over k whose function field is isomorphic to K. All properties of X can be derived from the function field.

Many questions can be dealt with on affine curves . Indeed, we can cover a projective curve X with affine open sets U_i which are themselves affine curves. So local constructions can be done on affine curves, whereas many global properties can be checked by checking them on all U_i. For example, checking whether a point on a curve is non-singular can be done in any open neighbourhood of this point.

It is of course important to be able to test whether a given curve X is non-singular or smooth. We illustrate how to do this for affine plane curves. We shall assume that $p = (0,0)$. Let f be an irreducible polynomial in x and y. One computes the linear part ℓ of the equation $f = 0$ near p. The equation $\ell = 0$ defines a linear subspace T of A^2. Then there is an isomorphism of vector spaces $T^* \cong m/m^2$ with m the maximal ideal of p and T^* the dual vector space of T. Indeed, by associating to $g \in k[X_1,X_2]$ its linear part one gets a map $d: k[X] \to Hom_k(T,k)$ with the properties i) $d(c) = 0$ for every $c \in k$, ii) $d(a+b) = d(a) + d(b)$, iii) $d(ab) = a(0)d(b) + b(0)d(a)$. We extend this by the formula

$$d(\tfrac{a}{b}) = \frac{b(0)d(a) - a(0)d(b)}{b(0)^2}$$

to a k-linear map $d: O_p \to T^*$. Restriction to $m \subset O_p$ gives the required isomorphism $m/m^2 \cong T^*$. This gives the connection with the more intuitive notion of tangent space (take the linear part of the equations). Hence if the linear part of f at the origin is non-zero, then $\dim_k T^* = 1$ and we have a non-singular point at the origin. For a projective curve given by f, the projective tangent space at $(p_0:p_1:p_2)$ is $f_X(p)X + f_Y(p)Y + f_Z(p)Z = 0$. If at least one of f_X,f_Y,f_Z is non-zero in p, then p is a smooth point. For example, the Fermat equation $X^n + Y^n + Z^n = 0$ defines a non-singular curve over k if char(k) does not divide n. The Klein quartic $X^3Y + Y^3Z + Z^3X = 0$ over $\mathbf{F}_p$ is non-singular unless $p=7$. Here the point $(1:2:4)$ is the only singular point.

3. If the field k is no longer algebraically closed, the Hilbert Nullstellensatz no longer holds in general since the corresponding points are lacking. For example, the equation $X^2+Y^2 = -1$ has no solutions over $\mathbf{R}$. Therefore, if we consider the case of an affine variety, it seems better to start with the coordinate ring instead of with a set of zeroes. So let $\bar{k}$ be an algebraic closure of k and let p be a prime ideal of $k[X_1,...,X_n]$ which generates a prime ideal $\bar{p}$ in $\bar{k}[X_1,...,X_n]$. Then $\bar{p}$ defines an affine variety X <u>defined over</u> k. A morphism of affine varieties over k is a morphism of the associated varieties over $\bar{k}$ which is given by a homomorphism of k-algebras. Similarly, a projective variety defined over k is given by a homogeneous prime ideal of $k[X_0,...,X_n]$ which remains prime when extended to $\bar{k}[X_0,...,X_n]$. To it we can associate a function field $k(X)$ by restricting our earlier definition to those pairs (U,f) where f can be defined by polynomials with coefficients in k. For a curve X this field is of the following shape : it contains k as a subfield and possesses an element x which is transcendental over k and such that k(X) is a finite algebraic extension of k(x). A field with these properties is called a field of algebraic functions of one variable over k. The elements of k are called the constants. By extending the constants to $\overline{k}$ we obtain the function field $\overline{k}$ (X).

We call X <u>smooth</u> if, after extension of k to an algebraic closure, the curve is a smooth curve.

We can view a curve X over k as a curve over $\overline{k}$ of which we can see only a fraction of all points. Now over $\overline{k}$ we had a 1-1-correspondence between the points of X and the discrete valuation rings of the function field. Since we cannot see all points, this does no longer hold, but we can look nevertheless at all discrete valuation rings contained in k(X) such that the discrete valuation is trivial on k. If v is a discrete valuation of k(X) and R_v is its valuation ring with maximal ideal m_v then $k_v = R_v/m_v$ is called the <u>residue field</u>. This is a finite extension of k. We call the pair (R_v, m_v) a <u>closed point</u> of X and d = $[k_v:k]$ the degree of the point. If k is algebraically closed then of course d=1 for every point. To a closed point of degree d over k we can associate a set of d points of degree one over $\overline{k}$ which are the conjugates of each other under Gal($\overline{k}$/k) : extend the discrete valuation v of k(X) to a discrete valuation of $\overline{k}$ (X). This corresponds to a point $P \in X$. These d points are all distinct if $\overline{k}$ /k is separable.

(1.8) Example. Let X = $\mathbb{P}^1$ over F_p . Every irreducible polynomial $f \in F_p[T]$ of degree $d \geq 1$ defines a closed point of degree d on $\mathbb{P}^1$. After extending F_p to F_{p^d} we can see the d points of degree one over F_{p^d} which form this point of degree one over F_p .

(1.9) Example.<u>The Klein Quartic</u>. Let $f = X^3Y + Y^3Z + Z^3X$ and let k = F_2. Over F_2 the curve defined by f = 0 has three points of degree one : (0:0:1), (0:1:0) and (1:0:0). Its points of degree 2 become visible over $F_4 = F_2[a]/(a^2+a+1)$: if we consider our curve as a curve over F_4 , then the curve has two more points of degree one : (1:a:1+a) and its conjugate (1:1+a:a). This pair of points defines a point of degree 2 on X over F_2. Over F_8 we find many more points. To describe these we first give a group of automorphisms of X over $F_8 = F_2[\zeta_7]$. An automorphism of order 7 over F_8 is given by α: (x:y:z) → (x:ζy:ζ^5z). Besides this we have an automorphism of order three: (x:y:z) → (z:x:y).(In fact, one can show that this curve admits G_{168}, the simple group with 168 elements as automorphism group.) Suppose that (x:y:z) is a point of X over F_8. If x≠0 and the point is not (1:0:0) then by applying α we can assume that both x and y are equal to 1. The condition is then: $1 + z + z^3 = 0$. There are three elements of F_8 satisfying this relation. Using the automorphisms we find 21 points. They come from 7 points of degree 3 over F_2. Together with the points over F_2 we already found we have 24 points over F_8. One can in fact give formulas for the number of points of x over F_{2k}.(See lecture 4 where this is explained.) The formula is : if $k \neq 0$ (mod 3) then N_k = # $X(F_{2k})$ equals $2^k + 1$; if $k = 0$ (mod 3) then N_k is given by $N_k = (1 + 2^k) - a_k$ with $a_{3k+6} + 5a_{3k+3} + 8a_{3k} = 0$. Moreover, $a_0 = 6$, $a_3 = -15$, $a_6 = 27$. Here is a small table.

k	1	2	3	4	5	6	9
N_k	3	5	24	17	33	38	528

We give a lemma that we need later. A field extension L/K is called separably generated over K if there exists an intermediate field K' which is a purely transcendental extension of K such that L/K' is separable algebraic (i.e. the minimum polynomial of every element of L over K' has distinct roots).

(1.10) Lemma. If the field k is perfect, then the field k(X) is separably generated over k.

Finite fields and fields of characteristic zero are examples of perfect fields.

References.

[1] Chevalley, C.: Introduction to the therory of algebraic functions of one variable. Math. Surv.,VI, New York, 1951.
[2] Fulton,W.: Plane algebraic curves.W.A.Benjamin,New York ,1969
[3] Hartshorne, R.: Algebraic Geometry .Graduate Texts in Math. 52. Springer Verlag, 1977. Ch. I,1-6.
[4] Shafarevich, I.: Basic algebraic geometry. Springer Verlag 1977. Ch. I, Ch. III.

II. Divisors on algebraic curves.

1. Let X be a smooth projective curve over k. A <u>divisor</u> is a formal linear combination

$$D = \Sigma \, n_P P$$

where the sum is over all closed points of X, the coefficients are integers and are almost always zero. We can add divisors formally and obtain a group : the group of divisors $\mathrm{Div}(X)$. A divisor is called <u>effective</u> if all n_P are non-negative. The <u>degree of a divisor</u> is

$$\deg(D) = \Sigma \, n_P \deg(P)$$

with $\deg(P) = [k_v : k]$ the degree of P. (Recall that $k_v = k(P)$ is the residue field of P, see Lecture 1.) The subgroup of divisors of degree zero is denoted $\mathrm{Div}_0(X)$.

Let f be a rational function on X. Then we define the divisor of f as

$$(f) = \Sigma \, v_P(f) \, P,$$

where v_P (or ord_P) is the discrete valuation associated to P. So we count the number of zeroes minus the number of poles with their multiplicities. For a given f in $k(X)^*$ we can assume-- after extending the field of constants if necessary -- that all points P in the divisor of f have degree one. Let $f : X \to Y$ be a non-constant morphism of non-singular projective curves. Let P be a point on Y and let t be a local coordinate at P. Let $P_1,...,P_r$ be the points on X lying over P. We define

$$f^*(P) = \Sigma_{i=1}^{r} \, v_{P_i}(f^*t) \, P_i \, .$$

This does not depend on the choice of t and is a finite sum. By linear extension we thus get a divisor $f^*(D)$ on Y for every divisor D on X : $f^*(\Sigma \, n_P P) = \Sigma \, n_P f^*(P)$. We call it the pull back of D under f.

Let $f \in k(X)$ be a rational function . We shall use the following theorem:

(2.1) Theorem. Let f be a non-constant morphism of non-singular projective curves. Let P be a closed point of Y. Then one has : $\deg f^*(P) = \deg f \cdot \deg P$ with $\deg f = [k(X) : k(Y)]$.

(2.2) Corollary. The degree of a divisor of a rational function f is zero.

Proof. Note that f defines a morphism $\phi : X \to \mathbb{P}^1$. Then one has : $\deg(f) = \deg \phi^*(0) - \deg \phi^*(\infty)$. ◊

To the smooth projective algebraic curve X we can now associate the group

$$\mathrm{Div}(X)/\{(f) : f \in k(X)^*\}.$$

This group is called the <u>divisor class group</u> and plays a crucial role in the theory of algebraic curves. It is denoted Pic(X). Its elements are the equivalence classes under the equivalence relation :

$D \approx D'$ if and only if $D' - D =$ divisor of a rational function.

This equivalence is called <u>linear equivalence</u>. Linearly equivalent divisors have the same degree. We shall discuss the divisor class group later.

Let D be a divisor on a curve X. We consider the following vector space over k :

$$L(D) = \{ \, f \in k(X)^* : (f) + D \geq 0 \, \} \cup \{0\}$$

where $\geq$ means : all coefficients are ≥ 0. That is, if we write $D = \Sigma_{i=1}^{r} \, n_i P_i - \Sigma_{i=1}^{r} m_i Q_i$

with all $n_i, m_i \geq 0$, we consider all functions f in the function field which have zeroes of order at least m_i at Q_i and that may have poles of order at most n_i at P_i. We claim : L(D) is a finite dimensional vector space over k .Indeed, first we observe that if D and D' are linearly equivalent then $L(D) \cong L(D')$ by $f \rightarrow fg$ if $(g) = D - D'$.

(2.3) Lemma. We have $L(D) = \{0\}$ if $\deg(D) < 0$ and $\dim_k L(D) \leq 1 + \deg(D)$ for $\deg(D) \geq 0$.

Proof. If $\deg(D) < 0$ then $\deg((f) + D) = \deg(D) < 0$ for any function $f \in k(X)^*$,so $L(D) = \{0\}$. If $\deg(D) \geq 0$ then either $L(D) = \{0\}$ or there exists a divisor $D' \geq 0$ with $D' \approx D$ (namely $D' = D + (f)$ for a function $f \neq 0$ in $L(D)$). Since $L(D) \cong L(D')$ we can replace D by D'. Therefore we may assume that $D = \Sigma_{i=1}^{m} \, n_i P_i$ with $n_i \geq 0$.An element of L(D) determines for i=1,...,m an element of $t^{-n_i} O_{P_i}/O_{P_i}$. This gives a linear map

$$\ell\colon L(D) \rightarrow \oplus_{i=1}^{m} \, t^{-n_i} O_{P_i}/O_{P_i}.$$

The kernel is k for if $\ell(f) = 0$ then $f \in O_{P_i}$ for all i and hence f is regular everywhere. But then f is constant. Hence

$$\dim_k L(D) \leq 1 + \Sigma_{i=1}^{m} \dim_k t^{-n_i} O_{P_i}/O_{P_i}$$

$$\leq 1 + \Sigma_{i=1}^{m} \, n_i \deg(P_i)$$

$$\leq 1 + \deg(D). \qquad\qquad \Diamond$$

The computation of the dimension $\ell(D)$ of $L(D)$ is known as the <u>problem of Riemann-Roch</u>. For more about this problem see later on. The projective space $\mathbb{P}(L(D))$ is denoted $|D|$. By associating

$$f \quad \rightarrow \quad (f) + D$$

one gets a bijection

$$|D| \longleftrightarrow \{ D' \in \text{Div}(X) : D' \approx D, D' \geq 0 \}.$$

The projective space $|D|$ is called the <u>complete linear system</u> associated to D, a projective linear subspace of $|D|$ is called a linear system. If D and D' are linearly equivalent then $L(D)$ is isomorphic to $L(D')$ via $f \rightarrow fg$ with g a function with divisor $D'-D$. Linear systems on curves are important because of their relation with morphisms. Let $V \subseteq L(D)$ be a linear subspace. Choose a basis $f_0, ..., f_n$ of V. Then we can define a rational map $X \rightarrow \mathbb{P}^n$ by : $x \rightarrow (f_0(x): ... :f_n(x))$, hence a morphism by (1.6). Conversely, let $f: X \rightarrow \mathbb{P}^n$ be a morphism such that the image is not contained in a hyperplane. Any hyperplane h $= 0$ in $\mathbb{P}^n$ cuts out a divisor on X. All these divisors are linearly equivalent.

2. Let X be an affine variety over k. We define a k[X]-module $\Omega[X]$ as follows. It is generated by elements df, $f \in k[X]$ with the relations: $d(f+g) = df + dg$, $d(fg) = fdg + gdf$, $da = 0$ for all $a \in k$. The elements of $\Omega[X]$ are called <u>regular differential forms</u>.

For a quasi-projective variety X, consider the following data: an open covering $\{U_i\}$ of X with affine open sets and a collection of regular differential forms $\omega_i \in \Omega[U_i]$ such that on the intersections $U_i \cap U_j$ we have $\omega_i = \omega_j$. We consider two such data $\{U_i, \omega_i\}$, $\{V_i, \eta_i\}$ equivalent if on all $U_i \cap V_j$ we have $\omega_i = \eta_j$. An equivalence class is called a <u>regular differential form</u>. For an affine variety this yields the same as before. We denote it again by $\Omega[X]$.

We can view a regular differential form as a rule which associates to each closed point x of X a linear function on the tangent space T_x ($= \text{Hom}_k(m/m^2, k)$). In fact if X is affine and $f \in k[X]$, then let $d_x f$ be the linear part of $f-f(x)$ in m/m^2. Then $x \rightarrow d_x f$ is such a rule defined by df.

(2.4) Example. Let X be a non-singular plane curve of degree d in $\mathbb{P}^2$ given by an affine equation $f = 0$. Then we can define regular differential forms on X (in affine coordinates X,Y) by

$$\omega = g \, dX/f_Y = -g \, dY/f_X ,$$

where g is an arbitrary polynomial of degree $\leq d-3$ in X,Y.(Note that we have $f_X dX + f_Y dY = 0$.) Working out the expression for ω in the other affine parts of $\mathbb{P}^2$ one sees that

48

the condition that the degree of $g \leq d-3$ is necessary and sufficient in order that the form ω is regular there.The dimension of the space of such polynomials g is

$$\binom{d-1}{2} = \frac{(d-1)(d-2)}{2} .$$

If P is a smooth point on a curve C, then there exists a neighbourhood U of P such that $\Omega[U]$ is a free $k[U]$-module with generator dt, where t is a local parameter in P.

In analogy with the definition of rational functions we can define the concept of a rational differential form: consider pairs (U,ω) with U a non-empty open set and ω a regular diffferential form on U. Define an equivalence relation

$$(U,\omega) \approx (V,\eta) \Leftrightarrow \omega = \eta \text{ on } U \cap V.$$

For an affine variety we find that the $k(X)$-module of rational differential forms equals $k(X) \cdot \Omega[X]$. It is generated by elements df with f in $k(X)$, where for g,h in $k(X)^*$ we have the rule $d(g/h) = (hdg - g\,dh)/h^2$.

(2.5) **Example**. Consider A^1 with coordinate X. On A^1 the expression dX defines a regular differential form. On $\mathbb{P}^1$ the pair (A^1,dX) defines a rational differential form. If $Y = \frac{1}{X}$ is a local coordinate near the point $(0:1)$ at infinity we have $dX = \frac{-1}{Y^2}dY$ and we see that the rational differential form is not regular on $\mathbb{P}^1$.

Two rational differential forms differ by a rational function on X. Hence the module of rational differential forms over $k(X)$ is of dimension 1 over $k(X)$. Another interpretation of this module is as the dual of the module of derivations. For all this we refer to [5].

Let ω be a rational differential form on a smooth curve.We can write near a closed point P the form ω as $\omega = fdt$ with $f = f_P$ a rational function and $t = t_P$ a local parameter. We can define the divisor of the differential form ω by

$$(\omega) = \Sigma_P \operatorname{ord}_P(f_P) P,$$

where ord_P is the valuation of the local ring O_P. The divisor class of a rational differential form on X is called the canonical divisor class of X and denoted by K .Often also a representative divisor is denoted by K. The canonical divisor class is well-defined because the quotient of two rational differential forms is a rational function on X. We can interpret the space $L(K)$, where K is the divisor of ω as a space of differential forms: by associating to $f \in L(K)$ the regular differential form $f\omega$ we get an isomorphism of k-vector spaces between $L(K)$ and the space $\Omega[X]$ of regular differential forms on X.

(2.6) Definition. Let X be a smooth projective curve defined over k. The dimension $\dim_k L(K)$ is called the <u>genus</u> g of X.

(2.7) Proposition. If X is a smooth projective curve over k and k_1/k is a separable field extension then the genus of X as a curve over k_1 equals the genus of X over k.

Since we shall work over finite fields we can and shall use this fact often .We refer to [1] for a proof.

Let P be a closed point on a smooth curve X and let ω be a rational differential form on X. We define the <u>residue of ω at P</u> as

$$\mathrm{res}_P\, \omega = \mathrm{Tr}\, a_{-1}\, ,$$

where we write ω as $\omega = \Sigma\, a_i\, t^i\, dt$ with t a local parameter at P and where Tr is the trace map from the residue class field $k(P)$ of P to k. Since the point is not necessarily of degree 1 we must take the trace to land in k. Of course, one must check that this definition is independent of the choice of a local parameter. This is a bit tedious but can be done; see [3] for a proof. A basic result from the theory of algebraic curves is the following theorem.

(2.8) Theorem. If ω is a rational differential form on a smooth projective curve, then the sum of the residues of ω is zero :

$$\Sigma_P\, \mathrm{res}_P\, \omega\ = 0,$$

where the sum is over all closed points of X.

The idea of the proof is to check this on $\mathbb{P}^1$ and then represent a curve as a branched cover of $\mathbb{P}^1$ and to check what happens under a morphism, see [3].

3. The famous theorem of Riemann-Roch gives a (partial) answer to the problem of Riemann-Roch.

(2.9) Theorem of Riemann-Roch. Let D be a divisor on a smooth projective curve X of genus g. Then

$$\dim_k L(D) - \dim_k L(K{-}D) = \deg(D) + 1 - g.$$

We do not prove this theorem here, but refer to the literature cited above for various proofs: [1], [2] ,[3] .

A divisor for which $L(K-D) \neq 0$ is called <u>special</u>.

(2.10) Corollary. We have $\deg(K) = 2g - 2$.

Proof. Take $D = K$. Then we find

$$\dim_k L(K) - \dim_k L(0) = \deg(K) + 1 - g.$$

But by definition $\dim_k L(K) = g$ and since everywhere regular functions are constant we have $\dim_k L(0) = 1$.

(2.11) Remark. Let D be a divisor of degree 1. Then $\dim L(D) \leq 1$ unless the genus $= 0$. Indeed, if $\dim L(D) \geq 2$ we take f, g linearly independent from $L(D)$. Then $Q \rightarrow (f(Q):g(Q))$ gives a morphism of X to $\mathbb{P}^1$ which is an isomorphism since any non–zero function from $L(D)$ has only one zero and one pole which implies by Theorem (2.1) that the degree of the morphism is one, i.e. $k(X) = k(\mathbb{P}^1)$.

(2.12) Definition. By a g_d^r we mean the linear system of effective divisors linearly equivalent to a given divisor D (i.e. $\mathbb{P}(L(D))$) with $r + 1 = \dim L(D)$ and $d = \deg(D)$.

(2.13) Definition. A curve X of genus $g \geq 2$ is called <u>hyperelliptic</u> if its function field has an involution i such that the fixed field of i is isomorphic to $k(x)$, the field of rational functions. Equivalently, if there is a morphism of degree two onto $\mathbb{P}^1$.

On a hyperelliptic curve there is a unique g_2^1 which is the pull-back of the unique g_1^1 on $\mathbb{P}^1$, i.e. the linar system of divisors $P+P'$, where P, P' are two points with the same image under the map of our curve to $\mathbb{P}^1$.

Let X be a smooth projective curve of genus $g \geq 2$. The functions in $L(K)$ with K a canonical divisor form a g-dimensional vector space and define a morphism

$$\phi : X \rightarrow \mathbb{P}^{g-1}$$

by $P \rightarrow (f_1(P): \ldots : f_g(P))$ with the f_i a basis of $L(K)$. In fact, by the Riemann-Roch theorem we can check that always one of $f_i(P)$ is non-zero: $\dim L(K-P) - \dim L(P) = g - 2$ and $\dim L(P) = 1$ by the remark above. So $\dim L(K-P) = g-1$. We find a well–defined morphism. Of course , it depends upon a choice of a basis. If f_i' is another basis and if ϕ' is the asssociated morphism then $\phi' = \phi \cdot g$ with g an automorphism of $\mathbb{P}^{g-1}$. Despite this element of choice, the morphism ϕ is called the <u>canonical map</u>. Suppose that ϕ identifies two different points, say P_1, P_2. Then $L(K-P_1) = L(K-P_1-P_2) = g-1$. By Riemann-Roch:

$$\dim L(K-P_1-P_2) - \dim L(P_1+P_2) = g - 3.$$

Hence $\dim L(P_1+P_2) = 2$. Then $L(P_1+P_2)$ defines a morphism of degree 2 on $\mathbb{P}^1$. A curve which admits a morphism of degree 2 onto $\mathbb{P}^1$ is a hyperelliptic curve. We see : the canonical map is injective if and only if X is not hyperelliptic. In fact, by applying the argument above also for $P_1 = P_2$ we find that if X is not hyperelliptic, then ϕ is an embedding (isomorphism onto its image).

As an example, take a curve of genus three which is not hyperelliptic. Then its image under the canonical map is a non-singular curve of degree 4 in $\mathbb{P}^2$.

4. In view of the theorem of Riemann-Roch it is important to be able to determine the genus of a curve. Let X be a non-singular projective algebraic curve of degree d in $\mathbb{P}^2$. Then one has the well-known <u>Plücker formula</u>:

$$g = \frac{1}{2}(d-1)(d-2).$$

For example, the Klein quartic has genus three if the characteristic is not 7(because the curve is singular in that case). A basis for the regular differential forms is given by (in affine form)

$$\omega_1 = XdX/f_Y = -XdY/f_X, \quad \omega_2 = YdX/f_Y = -YdY/f_X, \quad \omega_3 = dX/f_Y = -dY/f_X.$$

If the curve has mild singularities, then one still has a simple formula for the genus of a non-singular projective curve Y whose function field is isomorphic to $k(X)$. E.g. if X has only m ordinary double points (the mildest type of singular points : in an affine equation such that the singular point is $(0,0)$ the lowest order terms are quadratic and this defines a conic which is the union of two distinct lines) then

$$g = \frac{1}{2}(d-1)(d-2) - m .$$

Another way to determine the genus is to present X as a branched covering of another curve of which one knows the genus. So let $\phi : X \to Y$ be a non-constant morphism. The degree of ϕ is defined as $\deg\phi = [k(X):k(Y)]$, the degree of the field extension $k(X)/k(Y)$.

Let P be a closed point of X and let Q be its image. Choose a local parameter t
in Q. Using ϕ we can pull it back to an element of the local ring of P : $\phi^*t \in O_P$. We
define the <u>ramification index</u> e_P of ϕ at P as

$e_P = \text{ord}_P(\phi^*t)$.

If $e_P > 1$ then P is called a <u>ramification point</u> and Q is called a branch point. If char(k)
$= 0$ or   char(k) $= p > 0$ and p does not divide e_P then the ramification is called <u>tame</u>.
If char(k)$|e_P$ then we say that there is <u>wild ramification</u>.

Suppose now moreover that ϕ is separable (i.e. k(X)/k(Y) is a separable field
extension). We define the ramification divisor R on X as follows. Let dt   be the
differential of t at Q. Pull it back to X : ϕ^*dt. Then if s is a local parameter at P we
define

$r_P = \text{ord}_P(\phi^*dt/ds)$

and

$R = \Sigma_P\ r_P\,P$.

If the ramification is tame then $r_P = e_P - 1$, otherwise $r_P > e_P - 1$. The <u>Hurwitz-Zeuthen</u>
<u>formula</u> now computes the genus of X in terms of g(Y) and deg(R):

(2.14) Theorem. Let $\phi : X \rightarrow Y$ be a non-constant separable morphism of non-singular
projective curves. Then

$$2g(X) - 2\ =\ \deg(\phi)(2g(Y) - 2) + \deg R.$$

(2.15) Example. Let $k = F_2$, $Y = \mathbb{P}^1$ and let X be the non-singular projective curve
defined by the function field k(x,y) with $y^2 + y = x^5 + 1$. We have an involution $y \rightarrow y$
$+1$ on k(X) with fixed field $k(x) = k(\mathbb{P}^1)$. The field extension k(x,y)/k(x) corresponds
to a morphism ϕ of degree 2 : $X \rightarrow Y$.Restricted to the affine part A^1 with x as
coordinate we can give X by the affine equation $y^2 + y = x^5 + 1$ and ϕ by $(x,y) \rightarrow x$.
No closed point of A^1 is a branch point. The inverse image of $Q_\infty =(1:0) \in \mathbb{P}^1$ is the
point P_∞ which corresponds to the discrete valuation v_∞ with $v_\infty(x) = -2$, $v_\infty(y) = -5$. A
local parameter t at Q_∞ is 1/x, at P_∞ it is $s = x^2/y$. We have $d(y^2 + y) = d(x^5 + 1)$,
which gives $dy = x^4\ dx$. Since $v_\infty(x^2/y) = 1$, $v_\infty(d(x^2/y)) = 0$ we find $v_\infty(dy) = -6$,
$v_\infty(dx) = 2$. Therefore,

$r_{P_\infty} = v_\infty(d(1/x)/d(x^2/y)) = 6$.

Moreover, $r_P = 0$ for all other points P of X. We find

$g(X) = 2(-2) + 6 = 2$.

A basis for the 2-dimensional space of regular differentials is

dx, xdx.   ◊

5. Let Pic(X) be the group of divisor classes on a curve X. We have a surjective map

Pic(X) → $\mathbb{Z}$ [D] → deg(D).

whose kernel is denoted $Pic_0(X)$.

(2.16) Definition. An elliptic curve is a curve of genus one together with a point of degree one.

(2.17) Proposition. Let (E,P) be an elliptic curve over a field k. For every extension field K of k we have a bijection E(K) → $Pic^0(X)(K)$ given by Q →[Q–P]. Here E(K) (resp. $Pic^0(X)(K)$) denotes the set of K-rational points of E (resp. the group of divisor classes of degree zero defined over K).

Proof. Let D be a divisor of degree zero over K. Then D+P is a divisor of degree one. By the Riemann-Roch theorem L(D+P) has dimension 1. Hence there is a unique point Q over K with Q ≈ D + P. So the map is surjective. Suppose that Q and Q' have the same image. Then Q ≈ Q' and since dim L(Q) = 1 we find Q = Q'.   ◊

Using this proposition we can define on E an addition ⊕ such that E becomes a group with P as the identity element. Using the functions in L(3P) -- which is 3-dimensional -- we can map E to $\mathbb{P}^2$ such that the image is a non-singular curve of degree 3. We can normalize the equation such that it has the (affine) form (so-called Weierstrass form)

$$y^2 + a_1xy + a_3y = x^3 + a_2x^2 + a_4x + a_6 .$$

The identity element of the group is then (0:1:0). The addition is characterized by the fact that for any triple Q,R,S of points on E we have : Q⊕R⊕S = 0 in the group if and only if Q, R ,S are the three intersection points of E with a line given by L=0. Indeed, the line Z=0 cuts out on X the divisor 3P. The divisor of the function L/Z is Q+R+S-3P giving the relation Q⊕R⊕S = 0 . The converse is equally easy.

There is a vast literature on elliptic curves, see e.g. [4] .

References.

[1] Chevalley, C.: Introduction to the theory of algebraic functions of one variable. Math. Surv.,VI, New York,1951.

[2] Hartshorne, R.: Algebraic geometry. Graduate Texts in Math. 52. Springer Verlag 1977. Ch.Ch. I, Ch. IV.

[3] Serre,J-P.: Groupes algébriques et corps des classes. Hermann, Paris,1959. Ch. II.

[4] Silverman,J.: The arithmetic of elliptic curves. Graduate Texts in Math. 106. Springer Verlag 1986.

[5] Shafarevich,I.: Basic algebraic geometry. Springer Verlag 1977. Ch. I, Ch.III.

III.   Goppa Codes.

1. Let X be a non-singular projective curve defined over the finite field $\mathbf{F}_q$. Goppa had the beautiful idea of associating to a set of distinct points $P_1,...,P_n$ on X a code by evaluating a set of rational functions on X in the points P_i [see also Section 5 of Van Lint's lectures]. To be precise, let $P_1,...,P_n$ be rational points of X over $\mathbf{F}_q$ and set $D = P_1 + ... + P_n$. Let G be a divisor. We assume first that G has support disjoint from D (i.e. the points P_i occur with multiplicity 0 in G).

(3.1) Definition. The linear code $C(D,G)$ of length n associated to the pair (D,G) is the image of the linear map $\alpha: L(G) \rightarrow \mathbf{F}_q^n$ defined by

$$f \rightarrow (f(P_1),...,f(P_n)).$$

Such a code is called a <u>Goppa code</u>. Let us compute the parameters of this code. The dimension k of this code $C(D,G)$ is given by

$$k = \dim C(D,G) = \dim L(G) - \dim L(G - D).$$

Indeed, if f belongs to the kernel of α then $f \in L(G - D)$. The minimum distance d of $C(D,G)$ satisfies

$$d \geq n - \deg(G) .$$

Indeed, if the weight of $\alpha(f)$ is d then f vanishes in $n-d$ points P_j, so $(f) + G - P_{i(1)} - ... - P_{i(n-d)}$ is an effective divisor. By taking degrees : $\deg(G) - n + d \geq 0$.

Let us remark here that for reasons of degree: $\dim L(G - D) = 0$ if $\deg(G) < n$.

Remark. If G and D do not have disjoint support we still can associate a code to the pair (D,G), but no longer in a canonical way. We choose a rational function t on X such that $\text{ord}_{P_i} t = $ multiplicity of P_i in G. We then associate to f a code word via

$$f \rightarrow ((ft)(P_1),...,(ft)(P_n)).$$

If we choose a different t then we get an equivalent code, see (3.19).

There is a second code that we can associate to the pair (D,G). Let us define for a divisor E the vector space

$$\Omega(E) = \{ \omega : \omega \text{ a rational differential form with } (\omega) \geq E \} \cup \{0\}.$$

(3.2) Definition. The linear code $C^*(D,G)$ of length n associated to the pair (D,G) is the image of the linear map $\alpha^*: \Omega(G-D) \to F_q^n$ defined by

$$\eta \to (\mathrm{res}_{P_1}(\eta),...,\mathrm{res}_{P_n}(\eta)).$$

[Alternatively,since we can identify $\Omega(G-D)$ with $L(K+D-G)$ via $\eta \to \eta/\omega$, where ω is a fixed rational differntial form with divisor K, we can identify the image of α^* with the image of

$$\beta^*: L(K+D-G) \to F_q^n, \quad f \to (\mathrm{res}_{P_1}(f\omega),...,\mathrm{res}_{P_n}(f\omega)).]$$

Again let us compute the parameters of the code. The dimension k^* is given by

$$k^* = \dim L(K+D-G) - \dim L(K-G).$$

In particular, α^* is an injection if $\deg(G) > 2g-2$. For the minimum distance we find:

$$d^* \geq \deg(G) + 2 - 2g.$$

Indeed, suppose that $\alpha^*(f\omega)$ has Hamming weight d^*, i.e., $f\omega$ is regular in $n-d^*$ points $P_{i(1)},...,P_{i(n-d^*)}$. Then $f \in L(K+D - P_{i(1)} -...- P_{i(n-d^*)} - G)$, so $2g - 2 +n - (n-d^*) - \deg(G) \geq 0$.

(3.3) Proposition. The codes $C(D,G)$ and $C^*(D,G)$ are dual to each other.
Proof. For $f \in L(G)$ and $g\omega \in L(K+D-G)$ we have $\langle\alpha(f),\alpha^*(g\omega)\rangle = \Sigma_i \mathrm{res}_{P_i}(fg\omega) = \Sigma_{\mathrm{all}\ P}\, \mathrm{res}_P(fg\omega) = 0$ by the residue theorem, hence they are orthogonal.We have $k + k^* = \dim L(G) - \dim L(G-D) + \dim L(K+D-G) - \dim L(K-G) = n$ by the Riemann-Roch theorem. ◊

(3.4)Remark. Algebraic geometry tells us that there is an exact sequence

$$0 \to H^0(X,O(G-D)) \to H^0(X,O(G)) \to F_q^n \to H^1(X,O(G-D)) \to H^1(X,O(G)) \to 0.$$

We can identify this sequence with

$$0 \to L(G-D) \to L(G) \xrightarrow{\alpha} F_q^n \xrightarrow{\beta} \Omega(G-D)^* \to \Omega(G)^* \to 0,$$

where β is the dual of our map α^*. This explains the duality of codes. More explicitly :

(3.5) Lemma. There exists a <u>rational</u> differential form ω with simple poles with residue 1 in all P_i (i=1,...,n) such that $C^*(D,G) = C(D,K+D-G)$ with K the divisor of ω.
Proof. Let ω be a differential form as in the lemma. Then we have a commutative diagram:

$$\Omega(G{-}D) \rightarrow L(K{+}D{-}G)$$
$$\downarrow \alpha* \qquad \alpha \downarrow$$
$$F_q^n \quad = \quad F_q^n$$

where the upper arrow is an isomorphism which sends η to η/ω. The Riemann-Roch theorem tells us that a form ω as required exists. $\lozenge$

(3.6) Remark. This shows that the second construction gives the same class of codes as the first. In particular all results that we derive for the codes $C^*(D,G)$ can be carried over to the codes $C(D,G)$ and the reader can choose to work with the $C^*(D,G)$ or the $C(D,G)$ as he prefers. We shall mainly work with the $C^*(D,G)$.

(3.7) Example. Let X be the projective line $\mathbb{P}^1$ over F_q. We choose for D the $q{-}1$ points of $\mathbb{P}^1$ minus the origin P_0 and the point at infinity P_∞ and for G a multiple rP_∞ of the point at infinity. If we choose as basis for $L(G)$ the functions $1,t,...,t^r$ then the code is given by a matrix whose ij-th entry is α^{ij} with α a generator of the cyclic group F_q^*. The code $C(D,G)$ that we find is a so-called Reed-Solomon-code. This code is a MDS-code. In fact all Goppa codes obtained from curves of genus zero are optimal or MDS as we shall see in a moment. A variation : if we take for G a divisor of the form $rP_0 + sP_\infty$ we find examples of the so-called BCH-codes (as was first observed by Michon [3]).

(3.8) Remark. For the code $C(D,G)$ one has if $\deg(G) < n$:

$$k + d \geq n + (1 - g).$$

Indeed,we have $k = \dim L(G) - \dim L(G{-}D) = \deg(G)+1-g$ and $d \geq n-\deg(G)$
In terms of the invariants δ and R we thus have

$$\delta + R \geq 1 + (1 - g)/n.$$

In particular, for the codes coming from curves of genus zero, one has $n = k + d - 1$, i.e. the Singleton bound is reached. So we find :

(3.9) Corollary. If $g=0$ then $C(D,G)$ is optimal.

More generally, if we suppose that $\deg(G) \geq 2g{-}2$ we have (writing d for d^*) for the geometric Goppa code $C^*(D,G)$

$$\deg(G) + 2 - 2g \leq d \leq \deg(G) + 2 - g,$$

where the right hand side is the Singleton bound.

(3.10) Theorem. The minimum distance d of C*(D,G) is the smallest number of distinct points $P_{i(1)},...,P_{i(d)}$ from D such that in Pic(X) we have

$$G-K \approx \Sigma_{j=1}^{d} P_{i(j)} - Q,$$

where Q is an effective divisor on X with support disjoint from $P_{i(1)},...,P_{i(d)}$.

Proof. Let $f \in L(K+D-G)$ and suppose that there are exactly r points P_i, say $P_1,...,P_r$, where fω has a pole. Then we have

$$(f\omega) = -\Sigma_{i=1}^{r} P_i + G + E \quad \text{with } E \geq 0 ,$$

i.e. in terms of divisor classes

$$G - K \approx P_1 + ... + P_r - E. \qquad \qquad \Diamond$$

The special case g=1 of this theorem was treated by Driencourt and Michon in [4].

Another way of phrasing this is as follows. Let $D' \leq D$ be an effective divisor contained in D. Let r be the degree of D'. We have $L(K+D'-G) \subseteq L(K+D-G)$. If $L(K+D'-G) \neq \{0\}$ then C*(D,G) possesses a codeword of weight $\leq r$. To find the minimal distance we have to look at the divisor $D' \leq D$ of smallest (positive) degree such that $L(K+D'-G) \neq \{0\}$. Also the weight distribution can be read off from these spaces.For example, the number of code words with minimum distance d is (q–1) times the number of effective divisors $D' \leq D$ of degree d which are linearly equivalent to a divisor of the form $G-K+E$ with $E \geq 0$.

Dually, the code C(D,G) has minimum distance n–d where d is the maximum degree of a divisor D' with $0 \leq D' \leq D$ and $L(G-D') \neq 0$.

2. As we shall see, determination of the actual value of d or the number of code words with a given Hamming weight leads to very subtle questions on the geometry of the curve in question. We shall work this out in some detail for a number of curves.

(3.11) Example. Let X be the curve in $\mathbb{P}^2$ given by $X^3 + Y^3 + Z^3 = 0$. This curve has 3 points over F_2, 9 points over F_4, and 9 points over F_8. In fact the number of points over F_q with $q=2^r$ is 2^r+1 if r is not divisible by 2, and equals $2^{2k}+1 + (-1)^{k+1}2^{k+1}$ if r=2k. The nine points over F_4 are flex points and they give the points of order three in the group. Choose G as a point of degree 3 over F_2 (consisting of 3 new points Q_i (i=1,2,3) of degree one over F_8), and as D the sum of the nine points defined over F_4.

L(K+D–G) has dimension 6. We get a **[9,6,≥3]-code** C*(D,G) **over** F_4. The curve is an elliptic curve with origin (1:1:0). We have : d = 3 if and only if $Q_1 \oplus Q_2 \oplus Q_3$ = point of order three in the group. This is the case because this sum is a point over F_2 and all points over F_2 are points of order 3. The configuration of the nine points of order three has a large automorphism group : the group of affine transformations of $A^2(F_3)$.

(3.12) Example. Let X be the Klein quartic : $X^3Y + Y^3Z + Z^3X = 0$. We take for D the divisor consisting of all 24 points of X defined over F_8. Over F_4 there are two new points (of degree one). They define a point of degree 2 over F_2, call it B. They are the intersection points with the bitangent line X+Y+Z = 0. (A bitangent line is a line which is the tangent line for two distinct points of X.) Let G = mB with $3 \le m \le 11$ and take D = divisor of all points of X defined over F_8. We have for the code C = C*(D,G) :

n = 24, k = 26 – 2m, 2m + (2–g)≥ d ≥ 2m + (2–2g) with g=3.

If we take m=3, then d≥2. We have d=2 if and only if L(–B+D') ≠ {0} with D' ≤ D a divisor of degree 2. (Note that K ≈ 2B.) Suppose L(–B+D') ≠ {0}. Then the two points of D' are the two intersection points of a bitangent since 2D' ≈ K. But the points over F_8 are flex points, so the tangent there is not a bitangent.(A flex point is a point where the tangent has at least a threefold intersection with X .) So this is not possible and d≥3. Again, d=3 if and only if there exists a divisor D'≤ D of degree 3 with L(–B+D') ≠ {0}, i.e. there exists a point E (of degree one) over F_8 such that E + B ≈ D'. But then they belong to a g_3^1 and we can find a point Q over F_8 such that

E + B + Q ≈ D' + Q ≈ K.

(In fact, by Riemann-Roch one has dim L(D') – dim L(K–D') = 1, and we know dim L(D') ≥ 2, therefore dim L(K–D') ≥ 1.) This means that E + Q ≈ B, i.e. 2E + 2Q ≈ 2B ≈ K, i.e. E,Q are the two intersection points of a bitangent. But we do not have bitangents which are tangent in points rational over F_8. Therefore d≥4. By the Hamming bound d cannot be 5.

(3.13) Proposition. Let X be the Klein quartic $X^3Y + Y^3Z + Z^3X = 0$ in $\mathbb{P}^2$ over F_2. If B is the divisor of degree 2 over F_2 corresponding to the bitangent X+Y+Z = 0 and if D is the divisor consisting of all 24 flex points (defined over F_8) then the code C*(D,G) with G = 3B over F_8 has parameters **[24,20,4]**.

The fact that d≠5 implies that there exists a divisor D' with $0 \leq D' \leq D$ of degree 4 such that $L(D'-B) \neq \{0\}$, i.e. there exists an effective divisor E of degree 2 over F_8 such that $D' \approx B + E$. One can take $E = B$.

We can try to get good codes from this curve with G=mB and m ≥ 5. However, here one cannot improve above the minimum value for d :   **[n,k,d] = [24,26 - 2m, 2m – 4]**. In fact let us show this for m = 5 and for   m=11(see also (3.14)). Then $6 \leq d$ ≤ 9. We have d=6 if and only if there exists a divisor $0 \leq D' \leq D$ with $L(K+D'-5B) \neq \{$ $0 \}$., i.e. $D' \approx 3B$. This happens if and only if $D'+B \approx 2K$, i.e. there exists a conic which passes through B and the six points of D'. For suitable D' such a conic exists: XY + XZ + YZ = 0. So d = 6 for m=5. For m=11 we have d=18 if and only if there exists a divisor $D' < D$ of degree 18 with $G-K \approx 9B \approx D'$. Now $D \approx 6K \approx 12B$, therefore 9B $\approx D'$ if and only if $3B \approx D-D'$. As we saw above we can find such a D'.

By suitable concatenation one gets reasonably good codes over F_2. Indeed, applying a [4,3,2] -code, i.e. viewing each element of F_8 as a vector of length three over F_2 and replacing it by its image in F_2^4 under the linear map defined by the [4,3,2]-code,we obtain from the [24,20,4]-code over F_8 a **[96,60,8]**-code over F_2. This comes up to the world record for codes of this length.

The question whether a divisor class can be represented by an effective divisor D' < D is a subtle one. We give an example of a special case.

(3.14) Proposition. Let D be a divisor of degree 4 on the Klein curve over F_8 . Then there exist four distinct points (of degree one) such that D is linearly equivalent to their sum.

Proof. By Riemann-Roch dim L(D) = 1 or 2. If dim L(D) =2   then $D \approx K$ and the result is clear: take any four distinct points on a line. If dim L(D) = 1 and D is of the form $P_1 + g_3^1$ then since any g_3^1 can be written as a sum of three distinct P_i (different from

P_1) we are again done. If dim L(D) =1 and D is not of the form $P_1+ g_3^1$ then L(D) defines a map of degree 4 onto $\mathbb{P}^1$. If a fibre of this map contains four distinct P_i's we are done. If not, then each of the nine fibres contains at most three P_i's . If there are three F_8 -rational points in the fibre at least one of them must be a ramification point (otherwise the fourth point is also F_8 -rational). By the Hurwitz formula we can have at most six such fibres. On the other hand there must be six fibres with three P_i's (since there are 24 points P_i) and three fibres with two points of degree one over F_8. The fibre over a point over F_2 contains either only F_8-rational points defined over F_2 or contains three points rational over F_8 which are permuted transitively by the Frobenius morphism (which raises the coordinates to their second power) and are then all ramification points which is impossible. Therefore, the three fibres over points over F_2 can contain together only three points P_i, namely the F_2-rational points. This is a contradiction. ◊

Using this proposition one can determine the minimum distance for many codes $C^*(D,G)$. For example, if G is of degree 12 and D is as above, the sum of all F_8-rational points then $d = 8$. Indeed, $G-2K$ is of degree 4, hence can be written as sum of four distinct points $P_1+ ... +P_4$. Choose a line which intersects the Klein curve in four points $P_5,...,P_8$ of degree one distinct from $P_1...,P_4$. We have $G-K \approx P_1+ ... + P_8$, hence $d = 8$.

(3.15) Example. Let X be the hyperelliptic curve of genus 2 over F_2 defined by
$$Y^2 + Y = X^5 + 1.$$
(The genus can be computed by the Hurwitz-Zeuthen formula, see section 2.) It is a twofold cover of $\mathbb{P}^1$ ramified over the point at infinity. We denote by i the hyperelliptic involution. Let P_∞ be the point of X lying over the point at infinity. The number of points over F_{2^k} is $2^k + 1$ unless $k = 4m$. In that case the number of points over F_{2^k} is $2^{4m} + 1 + (-1)^{m+1}2^{2m+2}$. So over F_{2^4} we find 33 points : P_∞ and over each of the 16 points of the affine line two points P and $i(P)$. We now let $D = $ sum of all 32 points over F_{2^4} different from P_∞ and $G = mP_\infty$ with $m \geq 3$. For the code $C^*(D,G)$ we find $n = 32$, $k = 33 - m$ and $m - 2 \leq d \leq m$.

Suppose $d = m - 2$. We have : there exists a divisor $D' \leq D$ of degree $m - 2$ such that $D' \approx (m-2) P_\infty$. This is possible for m even by taking $(m-2)/2$ pairs of conjugate points. We now assume that m is odd. Then $D' \approx (m-2) P_\infty$ is impossible if $m = 3$ since X is not rational. Next let $m = 5$. We have: there exists a divisor $D' \leq D$ with $D' \approx 3P_\infty$. Then $2D' \approx 2K$. The hyperelliptic involution i acts as the identity on $|2K|$ since $L(2K)$ is generated by products of elements of $L(K)$, hence $2D'$ is a 2-canonical divisor invariant under the involution. But then also D' is invariant . This contradicts the fact that $\deg(D') = 3$. Next, let $m \geq 7$. Then we can find a D' with $D' \approx (m-2)P_\infty$. Indeed, the points lying over the 5 roots of 1 on the affine line with $Y=0$ form a divisor linearly equivalent with $5P_\infty$. By adding a suitable pair of two conjugate points $P + i(P)$ one gets a D' of the required form. We have proved:

(3.16) Proposition. Let X be the hyperelliptic curve over F_2 defined by $Y^2 + Y = X^5 + 1$ and let $G = mP_\infty$ with $3 \leq m \leq 31$ and let D be the sum of all points of X over F_{16} minus P_∞. Then the code $C^*(D,G)$ over F_{16} is of type **[32,33–m,d]** with **d = m–1** for **m = 3, 5** and **d = m–2** otherwise.

Let m=3 as in (3.16). We determine the number of code words with Hamming weight 2 . The number of code words of weight 2 equals 15 times the number of effective divisors $D' < D$ of degree 2 such that $D' \approx G{-}K + E \approx P_\infty + E$ for E a point distinct from D'. Then $|D'|$ is a g_2^1 , but on a curve of genus two there is only one g_2^1, namely

$|2P_\infty|$. We see that there are 16 such divisors D', all of the form $P + i(P)$ with $P \neq P_\infty$. We find $16 \cdot 15 = 240$ code words of Hamming weight 2 .

(3.17) Example. Let $q = p^{2k}, r = p^k$. Let X be the curve in $\mathbb{P}^2$ given by $X^{r+1} + Y^{r+1} + Z^{r+1} = 0$. On this curve we have an involution given by $(x:y:z) \rightarrow (x^r:y^r:z^r)$. Set $X' = X^{r+1}$ etc. This curve can then be written as $XX' + YY' + ZZ' = 0$, the so-called Hermite form. The genus of this curve is $g = (q - \sqrt{q})/2$. The number of rational points over F_q is $1 + q\sqrt{q}$. (So here the Hasse-Weil bound is reached, see next lecture.) We leave it as an exercise for the reader to determine the minimum distance for some codes $C^*(D,G)$ for the case $X^4 + Y^4 + Z^4 = 0$ over the field F_9.

3. Let us check what the self-duality of Goppa codes means. For this we introduce the following equivalence relation on linear codes in F_q .If C,C' are codes in F_q^n of the same dimension then we call them equivalent if there exists an element $a = (a_1,..,a_n) \in (F_q^*)^n$ such that $aC = C'$ (coordinate-wise multiplication).Note that this notion of equivalence differs from the one defined in Van Lint's lectures. In this section we shall use it only in the sense defined here. The following is obvious.

(3.18) Proposition. If two codes are equivalent then their weight distributions are equal.

$\Diamond$

(3.19) Proposition. Let $D = \Sigma P_i$ be a divisor on X as before and suppose that G , G' are linearly equivalent divisors with support disjoint from D. Then C(D,G) and C(D,G') are equivalent. Also C*(D,G) and C*(D,G') are equivalent.
Proof. Let $g \in k(X)$ with $(g) = G - G'$. In particular, $g(P_i) \neq 0$, i=1,...,n. Then we have an isomorphism

$$L(G) \rightarrow L(G'), \quad f \rightarrow fg.$$

This gives C(D,G') = aC(D,G) with $a_i = g(P_i)$. Similarly, the isomorphism

$$L(K+D-G) \rightarrow L(K+D-G'), \quad f \rightarrow fg$$

gives C*(D,G') = aC*(D,G).   ◊

Therefore, if we are only interested in the parameters n,k,d and the weight distribution of a code C (D,G) we can always replace G by a linearly equivalent divisor G' .

(3.20) Proposition. Suppose that $2G \approx K + D$. Then the code C(D,G) is equivalent to C*(D,G).
Proof. C*(D,G) equals C(D,K+D-G) with K as in the lemma above. But C(D,K+D-G) is equivalent to C(D,G).   ◊

Self-dual codes have been studied by Scharlau and by Stichtenoth , see [5],[6].

(3.21) Examples. The [32,16,15]-code over $\mathbf{F}_{16}$ obtained from the curve $Y^2 + Y = X^5 + 1$ is formally self-dual, i.e. equivalent to its own dual. Also the [24,12,10]-code obtained from the Klein quartic is formally self-dual.   ◊

The following theorem gives a sufficient condition for self-duality. For simplicity we shall assume that G and D have disjoint support.

(3.22) Theorem. Suppose that G > 0 and that deg(G) < n. Suppose that n = 2k and that there exists a diffferential form $\omega \in \Omega(2G-D)$ with $res_p(\omega) = 1$ for all P in D. Then C*(D,G) is self-dual.
Proof. If $\omega \in \Omega(2G-D)$ has residue 1 at all $P \in D$ then we have : $f\omega \in \Omega(G-D)$ for all $f \in L(G)$. But then $\alpha^*(f) = \beta^*(f\omega)$, so $C(D,G) \subset C^*(D,G) = C(D,G)^\perp$, and for dimension reasons $C(D,G) = C(D,G)^\perp$.   ◊

(3.23) **Remark.i)** The converse of the proposition (C(D,G) equivalent to C*(D,G) implies $2G \approx K+D$) does not hold.

ii) We can find a divisor class G such that $2G \approx K+D$ if and only if D is a square in Pic(X). This is a theorem of Weil, see [5].

4. It is not necessary to restrict to varieties of dimension 1. We give some examples of geometric codes obtained in an analogous way from higher-dimensional varieties.

(3.24) **Example.** Let $V = \{ f \in F_q[X_0,...,X_r], f$ homogeneous and linear$\}$. Obviously, $X_0,...,X_r$ consitute a basis. Let $P_1,...,P_n$ be all points of $\mathbb{P}^r(F_q)$, so $n=(q^{r+1} - 1)/(q-1)$ and define a code C as the image of $V \to F_q^n$ given by $X_i \mapsto X_i(P_j)$. We find a

$[n,r+1,q^r]$-code. This code is called a simplex code since all code words have the same distance. (Dual of the Hamming code; see also the Coding Theory part, Theorem 6.10) This code reaches the Plotkin bound: $A(n,d) \leq d/(d-\theta n)=q^{r+1}$.

(3.25) **Example.** Let $V = \{ f \in F_q[X_0,...,X_r] : f$ homogeneous of degree m$\}$. We have $\dim V= \binom{m+r}{m}$. Suppose $m \leq q$ and $P_1,..,P_n$ as in the previous example. Then the map $V \to F_q^n$, $f \to (...,f(P_i),...)$ is injective and defines a $[n,\binom{m+r}{m},d]$-code C with

$$d = n - M ,$$

where M = the maximal number of zeroes of $f \in V$.

Especially, if q=m=2, r=4 we find a **[31,15,8]-code** . In fact, the quadric with the maximum number of points over F_q is the reducible one consisting of two planes. It has $[15 + 15 - 7 = 23]$ points. So $d = 31 - 23 = 8$.

References.

[1] Goppa, V.D. : Codes and Information. Russian Math. Surveys 39, (1984), 87-141.

[2] Lachaud, G.: Les codes géometriques de Goppa. Sém. Bourbaki 37 ème année,1984-85,n° 641.

[3] Michon,J.-F.: Les codes BCH comme codes géométriques.

[4] Michon, J.-F., Driencourt,Y.: Remarques sur les codes géométriques. C.R. Acad. Sci. Paris, t. 301, Série I, n° 1, 1985.

[5] Scharlau, W.: Selbst-duale Goppa-Codes. Preprint, 1987.

[6] Stichtenoth, H.: Self-dual Goppa codes. To appear in Journal Pure and Appl. Algebra.

IV. Counting points on curves over finite fields

1. The zeta function of a curve over a finite field.

The classical Riemann zeta function

$$\zeta(s) = \Sigma_{n=1}^{\infty} n^{-s} \qquad (s \in \mathbb{C})$$

is well-known. It converges for $\mathrm{Re}(s) \geq 1$ and can be extended to a meromorphic function of s with a simple pole $s=1$. We can also write it as

$$\zeta(s) = \Pi_p (1 - p^{-s})^{-1}, \qquad \text{(Euler product)}$$

where the product is over all primes (of $\mathbb{Q}$). We can define a similar function for the function field $k(X)$ of a smooth projective curve X over a finite field $\mathbb{F}_q$. Indeed, define formally

$$\zeta(X,s) = \Pi_P (1 - N(P)^{-s})^{-1}$$
$$= \Sigma_{D \geq 0} N(D)^{-s} = \Sigma_{D \geq 0} q^{\deg(D)(-s)}.$$

Here $s \in \mathbb{C}$. (For convergence see later.) Here the product is taken over all closed points P of X and $N(P) = \# k(P) = q^{\deg(P)}$ and the sum is over all non–negative divisors on X and $N(D) = q^{\deg(D)}$. For example, if $X = \mathbb{P}^1$ and $q=p$ then

$$\zeta(X,s) = (1 - p^{-s})^{-1} (1 - p^{-s+1})^{-1}.$$

We define

$$\delta = \text{g.c.d. of all degrees of effective divisors on } X,$$

and

$$h = \# \mathrm{Pic}_0(X).$$

If there exists a divisor D' of degree m then $\# \mathrm{Pic}_m(X) = \# \mathrm{Pic}_0(X)$ (via $D \to D + D'$). The number a_n of effective divisors of degree n is given by

$$\underset{[D] \in \mathrm{Pic}_n(X)}{\Sigma} \frac{q^{\dim L(D)} - 1}{q - 1}.$$

Moreover, if $n > 2g-2$ and n is a multiple of δ, then by Riemann-Roch this number is

$$a_n = h \frac{q^{n+1-g} - 1}{q - 1}.$$

We can write

$$\zeta(X,s) = Z(X, q^{-s})$$

which defines a power series $Z(X,t)$. It converges for $|t| < q^{-1}$ (equivalently, $\mathrm{Re}(s) > 1$). We have

$$Z(X,t) = \Sigma_{n=0}^{2g-2} a_n t^n + \Sigma_{n=e}^{\infty} a_{n\delta} t^{n\delta}$$

(with $e = (2g-2+\delta)/\delta$, so that $e\delta$ = smallest multiple of δ larger than $2g-2$)

$$= \text{polynomial} + \frac{h'}{q-1} \Sigma_{n=e}^{\infty} (q^{n\delta+1-g}-1)\, t^{n\delta}.$$

But

$$\Sigma_{n=e}^{\infty} (q^{n\delta+1-g}-1)\, t^{n\delta} = \frac{q^{g-1+\delta}t^{2g-2+\delta}}{1-(qt)^{\delta}} - \frac{t^{2g-2+\delta}}{1-t^{\delta}}.$$

So we get a rational function of t. We observe that it has poles of order 1 when $t^{\delta} = 1$ and $t^{\delta} = q^{-\delta}$.

Another expression for the function $Z(X,t)$ is given by

$$\log Z(X,t) = \Sigma_{r=1}^{\infty} N_r t^r / r, \tag{1}$$

with N_r the number of points (of degree one) of X over $\mathbf{F}_{q^r}$. This follows immediately from the definition $\zeta(X,s) = \prod_P (1-N(P)^{-s})^{-1}$. It is convenient to view the points over $\mathbf{F}_{q^r}$ as the fixed points of F^r with F the Frobenius morphism on X which raises the coordinates of a point to their q-th power.

The following theorem describes some very strong properties of $Z(X,t)$.

(4.1) Theorem. i) The function $Z(X,t)$ is a rational function of t.

ii) $Z(X,t)$ satisfies a functional equation:

$$Z(X,q^{-1}t^{-1}) = q^{1-g}t^{2-2g}Z(X,t).$$

iii) We have the factorization:

$$Z(X,t) = \frac{P_1(t)}{P_0(t)P_2(t)},$$

where $P_0 = 1-t$, $P_1 = 1-qt$, $P_1 = \prod_{i=1}^{g}(1-\alpha_i t)(1-\bar{\alpha}_i t)$ with α_i $(i=1,...,g)$ algebraic integers of absolute value $q^{1/2}$.

Part i) was shown above. Also part ii) is an easy consequence of the Riemann-Roch theorem on X. In fact, one first proves the following lemma.

(4.2) Lemma. Let $Z_n(X,t) = Z(X/F_{q^n},t)$. Then

$$Z_n(X,t^n) = \prod_{\zeta} Z(X,\zeta t),$$

where the product is over all n-th roots ζ of 1.

If one takes $n = \delta$ then, since $Z(X,t) = \Sigma\, a_{n\delta}t^{n\delta}$ we have $Z(X,\zeta t) = Z(X,t)$, hence $Z_{\delta}(X,t^{\delta}) = Z(X,t)^{\delta}$. Now $Z_{\delta}(X,t^{\delta})$ has a pole of order 1 at $t = 1$ and $Z(X,t)^{\delta}$ has a pole of order δ in $t = 1$, hence $\delta = 1$.

We now have

$$Z(X,t) = \sum_{n=0}^{\infty} a_n t^n = \sum_{n=0}^{2g-2} a_n t^n + \sum_{n=2g-2}^{\infty} a_n t^n$$

$$= \sum_{D \in \text{Pic}(X),\, 0 \le \deg(D) \le 2g-2} \frac{q^{\dim L(D)} - 1}{q-1} t^{\deg(D)} - \frac{h}{q-1} \cdot \frac{t^{2g-1}}{1-t} +$$

$$+ \frac{h}{q-1} \cdot \frac{q^{1-g}(qt)^{2g-1}}{1-qt} \quad .$$

So we have

$$(q-1)Z(X,t) = \sum_{n=0}^{2g-2} t^n \sum_{\deg(D)\,=\,n} q^{\dim L(D)} + h\{q^{1-g} \frac{(qt)^{2g-1}}{1-qt} - \frac{1}{1-t}\} \ .$$

Applying Riemann-Roch to this identity one easily deduces ii) of the theorem. Indeed, if we replace t by $t^{-1}q^{-1}$ and multiply by $q^{1-g}t^{2g-2}$, the two terms between the brackets { } are interchanged, while $t^n q^{\dim L(D)}$ goes to $t^{2g-2-n} q^{\dim L(K-D)}$ by Riemann-Roch.

Part iii) lies deeper. It is a consequence of the analogue of the Riemann hypothesis for curves over finite fields proved by Weil using intersection theory on the surface $X \times X$. Another proof using only Riemann-Roch was given by Stepanov, see [1]. Weil proved that

$$N_r - (1+q^r) = a_r \text{ with } |a_r| \le 2g\sqrt{q^r}. \qquad \text{(The Hasse-Weil bound)}$$

It follows from this that if we write

$$\log Z(X,t) = \sum_{i=1}^{g} \log (1-\alpha_i t) + \sum_{i=1}^{g} \log (1-\bar{\alpha}_i t) - \log (1-t) - \log(1-qt),$$

we have using (1)

$$N_r = q^r + 1 - \sum_{i=1}^{g} (\alpha_i^r + \bar{\alpha}_i^r)$$

and we have $|\alpha_i| \le \sqrt{q}$ for all i. The functional equation then implies $|\alpha_i| = \sqrt{q}$ .By computing α_i we thus can determine N_r for all r.

For example, if $g=1$ and we know N_1 , then we know $\alpha_1 + \bar{\alpha}_1$.Using $\alpha_1 \bar{\alpha}_1 = q$ we find α_1 and $\bar{\alpha}_1$. Hence we then know the number of points over all extension fields of F_q. For higher genus one has to compute more N_r in order to determine all α_i. For example, consider the Klein quartic. Over F_2 there are three points as one can easily check. Over F_4 one finds 2 more points. Using the automorphism group one determines the number of points over F_8 ; it is 24. These are the flex points. With this information and using the functional equation one determines the shape of the zeta function of the Klein quartic over F_2 :

$$Z(X,t) = \frac{1+5t^3+8t^6}{(1-t)(1-2t)} \ .$$

Another example. Let X be the hyperelliptic curve $Y^2 + Y = X^5 + 1$ over F_2. We find 3 points over F_2 and 5 points over F_4. This determines the α_i : $\alpha_1 = 1 + i$, $\alpha_2 = -1 + i$. The shape of the zeta function is

$$Z(X,t) = \frac{(1+2t-2t^2)(1+2t+2t^2)}{(1-t)(1-2t)} .$$

[Remark. The numbers α_i that come up here have an intrinsic meaning: they are the eigenvalues of the operator induced by the Frobenius morphism on the first etale cohomology group of our curve, see Hartshorne for references. Part iii) of Theorem (4.1) is now analogous to the Lefschetz fixed point theorem in topology, where one expresses the number of fixed points of an automorphism by means of the trace of the induced operator on the (co)homology, see [8].]

One strategy for producing good codes with the help of algebraic curves is by taking a curve X over a fixed field F_q with a lot of rational points, say $P_1,...,P_n$ and then by putting $G = mP_n$ and $D = P_1+...+P_n$. This produces codes with

$d+k \geq n + 1 - g$

i.e. with

$$\delta + R \geq 1 + (\frac{1-g}{n}) .$$

In order to maximize the yield asymptotically, one looks for a family of curves X with $N(X) = N_1(X)$ as large as possible. We define

$$A(q) = \lim \sup_X \frac{N(X)}{g(X)} ,$$

where X runs over all smooth projective curves over F_q (up to isomorphism over F_q). From the Hasse-Weil bound we deduce immediately

$$A(q) \leq 2\sqrt{q} .$$

Ihara improved this bound as follows.

(4.3) Theorem.(Ihara [2]). We have $A(q) \leq \frac{\sqrt{8q+1}-1}{2}$.

Proof. The idea is very simple: if the α_i have argument near $-\pi$ then N_1 is big; but then the squares of the α_i have arguments near 2π , hence N_2 is small. However, we have $N_1 \leq N_2$. More formally, set $a_i = \alpha_i + \bar{\alpha}_i$. Then

$$q+1 - \Sigma_{i=1}^g a_i = N_1 \leq N_2 = q^2 + 1 + 2qg - \Sigma_{i=1}^g a_i^2 .$$

By the Schwarz inequality

$$g \cdot \Sigma_{i=1}^{g} a_i^2 \geq (\Sigma_{i=1}^{g} a_i)^2$$

we get

$$N_1 \leq q^2 + 1 + 2qg - g^{-1}(N_1 - q - 1)^2$$

i.e.

$$N_1^2 - (2q+2-g)N_1 + (q+1)^2 - (q^2+1)g - 2qg \leq 0.$$

Hence we see

$$2N_1 \leq \sqrt{(8q+1)g^2 + (4q^2 - 4q)g} - (g - 2q - 2)$$

which implies

$$\limsup \frac{N_1}{g} \leq \frac{1}{2} \{\sqrt{8q+1} - 1\}. \qquad \diamond$$

This bound was improved by Vladut and Drinfeld (using similar ideas) to :

(4.4) Theorem.(Vladut-Drinfeld [5]) One has $A(q) \leq \sqrt{q} - 1$.

One can show using modular curves that this bound is exact for even prime powers : $q = p^{2m}$, see next lecture. Manin conjectured

(4.5) Conjecture (Manin [4]) One has $A(p^{2m+1}) = p^m - 1$.

Serre proved that $A(q) > 0$. In fact, he proved that there exist a constant $c > 0$ with $A(q) > c \log q$.

Let $N_q(g)$ be the maximum number of points on a curve of genus g over $\mathbf{F}_q$. (Do not confuse this notation with $N_i(X)$.) By the Hasse-Weil bound one has

$$N_q(g) \leq q + 1 + [2g\sqrt{q}]$$

This can be improved as was shown by Serre :

$$N_q(g) \leq q + 1 + g[2\sqrt{q}].$$

By a variety of methods $N_q(g)$ can be determined for low genera and for various q. We give a sample of the results from Serre's papers [6,7] :

Let $q = p^e$ with $e \geq 1$, $m = [2\sqrt{q}]$.

g=1.

$$N_q(1) = q+m \qquad \text{if } e \text{ odd}, e \geq 3, \text{ and } p \text{ divides } m$$
$$N_q(1) = q+m+1 \qquad \text{otherwise.}$$

g=2.

$$N_q(2) = q+1+2m \qquad \text{unless if } q \text{ satisfies one of the following}$$

q = 4, 9,

q not a square, p divides m,

q not a square, of the form x^2+x+1 or x^2+x+2 with $x \in \mathbb{Z}$.

In these exceptional cases $N_q(2) = q + 2m$ or $q+2m-1$ or $q+2m-2$ (only if q=4).

A table for small q :

q	2	3	4	5	7	8	9	11	13	16	17	19	23	25	27
$N_q(1)$	5	7	9	10	13	14	16	18	21	25	26	28	33	36	38
$N_q(2)$	6	8	10	12	16	18	20	24	26	33	32	36	42	46	48
$N_q(3)$	7	10	14	16	20	24	28	28	32	38	40	44	?	56	?

Of course one can also keep q fixed and vary g. For q=2 a table of results :

g	=	0	1	2	3	4	5	6	7	8	9	15	19	21	39	50
$N_2(g)$	=	3	5	6	7	8	9	10	10	11	12	17	20	21	33	40.

We see in particular that the Klein curve over $\mathbb{F}_8$ has the maximum number of points : 24. The Hermite curves over $\mathbb{F}_q$ form a class of curves for which

$$\# X(\mathbb{F}_q) = q+1+gm. \tag{2}$$

Curves for which (2) holds are called maximal. See [3] for other examples of maximal curves.

If one knows the zeta function

$$Z(X,t) = \frac{\Pi_{i=1}^{g}(1-\alpha_i t)(1-\bar{\alpha}_i t)}{(1-t)(1-qt)}$$

of a curve X over $\mathbb{F}_q$ then one also can determine the number of points on the jacobian of X over $\mathbb{F}_q$. This can be useful for the determination of the minimum distance as in Lecture 3 and we just state the result.

(4.6) Proposition. The number of points of $\text{Pic}_0(X)(\mathbb{F}_{q^r})$ equals

$$\Pi_{i=1}^{g}(1-\alpha_i^r)(1-\bar{\alpha}_i^r).$$

(4.7) **Example**. Working this out for the jacobian of the Klein curve over F_2 we find for
$J_r = \#Pic_0(X)(F_{2^r})$: $J_r = 8^r + 1 - \frac{1}{3}a_{3r}$ if $r \neq 0 \pmod 3$ and $J_{3r} = (J_r)^3$. Here the
a_k are integers defined by the recurrence relation :

$$a_{3k+6} + 5a_{3k+3} + 8a_{3k} = 0 \quad \text{and} \quad a_3 = -15, \, , a_6 = 27 \, .$$

So $J_1 = 14, J_2 = 56, J_3 = 14^3$.

References.

[1] Bombieri ,E.: Counting points on curves over finite fields [d'après Stepanov]. Sém. Bourbaki, 25 ème année,1972/73, n° 430.

[2] Ihara,Y. : Some remarks on the number of rational points of algebraic curves over finite fields. J. Fac. Sci. Univ. Tokyo, Sec. Ia, 28, n° 3, 721-724 (1982).

[3] Lachaud,G.: Sommes d'Eisenstein et nombre de points de certaines courbes algébriques sur les corps finis. C.R. Acad. Sci. t. 305, Série I, p. 729-732 (1987).

[4] Manin, Yu.I.: What is the maximal number of points on a curve over F_2 ? J. Fac. Sci. Univ. Tokyo, Sec. Ia,28, N° 3, 715-720 (1982).

[5] Vladut, S.G., Drinfel'd, V.G.: Number of points of an algebraic curve. Funct. Anal. Vol. 17, N° 1, 68-69 (1983).

[6] Serre, J.-P.: Sur le nombre des points rationnels d'une courbe algébrique sur un corps fini. C.R. Acad. Sci. Paris,t. 296,Série I, 1983,p.397-402; = Oeuvres, III, n° 128, 658-663.

[7] Serre, J.-P.: Nombre de points d'une courbe algébriques sur F_q . Sém. Th. Nombres, Bordeaux, 1982-1983, exp. n°. 22; = Oeuvres, III, n° 129,p.664-66.

[8] Weil, A.: Number of solutions of equations in finite fields. Bull. Amer. Math. Soc., 55,1949,p.497-508; = Oeuvres Scient.,I,1949 b,p.399-410.

V. Shimura curves and codes.

1. One of the problems of coding theory is to find codes over the field F_q for which the ratios $\frac{d}{n}$ and $\frac{k}{n}$ (with d the minimum distance, k the dimension and n the word length) are as large as possible. To a (linear) code we can associate a pair (δ,R) with $\delta = d/n$, $R = k/n$ in the unit square $[0,1]\times[0,1]$. We consider the set V_q of all such pairs (δ,R) obtained from linear codes and we let U_q be the set of limit points of V_q. Manin proved the following theorem about U_q, see [5,6].

(5.1) Theorem. There exists a continuous function $\alpha_q : [0,1] \rightarrow [0,1]$ such that
$$U_q = \{ (\delta,R) : 0 \le \delta \le 1, \ 0 \le R \le \alpha_q(\delta) \}.$$
Moreover, $\alpha_q(0) = 1$ and α_q is strictly decreasing on the interval $[0,\frac{q-1}{q}]$ and vanishes on $[\frac{q-1}{q},1]$ (by the Plotkin bound). For $0 \le \delta \le \frac{q-1}{q}$ we have
$$\beta_q(\delta) \le \alpha_q(\delta) \le 1 - \frac{q}{q-1}\delta \,,$$
where β_q is the entropy function
$$\beta_q(\delta) = 1 - \frac{\delta\log(q-1) - \delta\log q - (1-\delta)\log(1-\delta)}{\log q} \,.$$

The curve $(\delta,\beta_q(\delta))$, $\delta \in [0,1]$ is called the Gilbert-Varshamov curve.

(5.2) Lemma. If one has a sequence $\{X_i : i \in \mathbb{Z}\}$ of non-singular projective curves over F_q such that $g_i = g(X_i)$ tends to infinity and such that $\lim_{i \to \infty} \frac{g_i}{N_1(X_i)} = \gamma$ then the line $\delta + R = 1 - \gamma$ is contained in U_q.

Proof. Let (δ,R) be a point on this line. One takes divisors G_i of degree $N_1(X_i)(1-\delta)$. This gives codes with invariants (δ_i,R_i). The efficiency of the resulting code R_i tends to $(1-\delta) - \gamma$. On the other hand we know from (3.8) that $R_i + \delta_i \ge 1 + \frac{1-g_i}{N_1(X_i)}$. Together with (5.1) this proves the result. ◊

In order to produce a family of good Goppa codes for which $R + \delta$ comes above the Gilbert-Varshamov line one needs a family of curves with a lot of rational points compared to the genus. The so-called modular curves or Shimura curves give an example of such a family of curves. We give a sketch of the ideas but must refer to the literature for a more detailed treatment of the deep theory of these curves.

A moduli space is roughly speaking a variety whose points classify the isomorphism classes of some kind of objects, e.g. algebraic curves of a certain type. It is natural here to look at such modular curves in connection with Goppa codes since their points have an interpretation. The modular curves we shall be concerned with are moduli spaces of elliptic curves.

2. We start with elliptic curves defined over a given field k. We are interested in the set of isomorphism classes of elliptic curves over this field. As we saw in lecture 2 we can present our elliptic curve E by the so-called (affine) Weierstrass form

$$y^2 + a_1xy + a_3y = x^3 + a_2x^2 + a_4x + a_6 .$$

The point P corresponds to $(0:1:0)$. Indeed, we have by Riemann-Roch $\dim L(2P) = 2$, $\dim L(3P) = 3$. Choose in $L(2P)$ a function x with a double pole at P, and choose in $L(3P)$ a function y with a triple pole at P. Since $\dim L(6P) = 6$, there must be a linear relation between the functions $1, x, y, xy, x^2, y^2, x^3$. This gives (after normalization) the equation above.

We can define invariants of E by

$$b_2 = a_1^2 + 4a_2 , \quad b_4 = a_1a_3 + 2a_4 , \quad b_6 = a_3^2 + 4a_6 , \quad c_4 = b_2^2 - 24b_4 ,$$

$$\Delta = -b_2^2b_8 - 8b_4^3 - 27b_6^2 + 9b_2b_4b_6,$$

and

$$j = \frac{c_4^3}{\Delta} .$$

The fact that E is non-singular is equivalent to $\Delta \neq 0$. A Weierstrass equation for the elliptic curve is unique up to coordinate changes of the form :

$$x \rightarrow u^2x' + r, \quad y \rightarrow u^3y' + su^2x' + t$$

with r, s, t, u in k and $u \neq 0$. Under such a change of coordinates we find $j = j'$. If two elliptic curves are isomorphic then $j = j'$. Conversely, if k is algebraically closed and $j = j'$ then E and E' are isomorphic. So over an algebraically closed field k the isomorphism classes of elliptic curves are in 1-1 correspondence with the points of the affine line A^1 with coordinate j. We say that A^1 is the moduli space of elliptic curves over k. [For the precise definition of the notion moduli space see [3]]. That j does not suffice to specify an elliptic curve if k is not algebraically closed is due to the fact that an elliptic curve can have a non-trivial automorphism group.

To get more moduli spaces we consider pairs (E,G), where E is an elliptic curve and where G is a cyclic subgroup of order N in E . Let us first look at the possibilities for these cyclic subgroups.

Let E be an elliptic curve. We set E[N] for the kernel of multiplication by N. If N is the product N_1N_2 of two coprime numbers N_1, N_2 then E[N] = E[N_1]×E[N_2]. Now let p be a prime. Then the morphism [p]: E $\to$ E which is multiplication by p (in the group) has degree p^2. If p $\neq$ char(k) then E[p] consists of p^2 points and is isomorphic (as group) to $\mathbb{Z}/p\mathbb{Z} \times \mathbb{Z}/p\mathbb{Z}$. If p = char(k) then multiplication by p is an inseparable morphism. There are two possibilities : either the degree of inseparabilty is p and E[p] consists of p points and is isomorphic to $\mathbb{Z}/p\mathbb{Z}$ or the degree of inseparablity is p^2 and E[p] consists of one point. In the former case we say that E is ordinary, in the latter case we say that E is a <u>supersingular</u> elliptic curve.

3. The existence of good codes coming from modular curves is based upon three facts :
i)   the existence of modular curves,i.e. curves whose points have an interpretation,
ii) the fact that the zeta function of such curves is known. This is due to the modular interpretation of our curves. We can express the number of points (over $\mathbf{F}_{p^2}$) in terms of a trace of a certain operator on a space of differential forms.
iii) the trace formula, which computes the trace of a Hecke operator on the space of modular forms. This is the trace mentioned in ii).

We shall try to explain the main points. To begin with we have:

(5.3) Theorem. There exists a curve $X_0(N)$ defined over $\mathbb{Z}[\frac{1}{N}]$ which is the moduli space of pairs (E,G) where E is an elliptic curve and G is a cyclic subgroup of order N.

Roughly speaking this means the following.[We stress that this is only a rough approximation. One needs the concept of a scheme. For more details, see [3].] There exists an algebraic curve whose equations have coefficients in $\mathbb{Z}[\frac{1}{N}]$ such that for every prime p the following holds. If we reduce the equations of $X_0(N)$ modulo p, we get a non-singular curve over $\mathbf{F}_p$ whose points over an algebraic closure k of $\mathbf{F}_p$ correspond 1-1 to the isomorphism classes of pairs (E,C) with E an elliptic curve over k and C a cyclic subgroup of E of order N. Moreover, if we extend scalars to $\mathbb{C}$,i.e. if we consider the complex curve defined by the equations of $X_0(N)$, then again its points correspond 1-1 to the pairs (E,C) where E is a complex elliptic curve and C a cyclic subgroup of order N.

Over the complex numbers we can give a very explicit description of $X_0(N)$. A complex elliptic curve E can be described as a torus : $E = \mathbb{C}/\mathbb{Z} + \mathbb{Z}\tau$ with τ in $\mathbb{C}$ but not in $\mathbb{R}$. Replacing τ by $-\tau$ if necessary we can assume that τ has positive imaginary part, i.e. lies in the upper half plane H. Two elliptic curves $E = \mathbb{C}/\mathbb{Z} + \mathbb{Z}\tau$ and $E = \mathbb{C}/\mathbb{Z} + \mathbb{Z}\tau'$ are isomorphic (as elliptic curves) if and only if there exists an element $\begin{pmatrix} a & b \\ c & d \end{pmatrix}$ in $SL(2,\mathbb{Z})$ such that

$$\frac{a\tau+b}{c\tau+d} = \tau'.$$

Therefore, the isomorphism classes of elliptic curves over $\mathbb{C}$ correspond 1-1 to the points of the orbit space $H/SL(2,\mathbb{Z})$, where the action is given by

$$\tau \to \frac{a\tau+b}{c\tau+d}.$$

A fundamental domain for this action of $SL(2,Z)$ on H is given by

$$F = \{\, z \in H : |z| \geq 1,\ |Re(z)| \leq \tfrac{1}{2} \,\}.$$

The function $z \to j(\mathbb{C}/\mathbb{Z} + \mathbb{Z} z)$ identifies the fundamental domain (with the appropriate identifications on the boundary) with $\mathbb{C}$. The function field of $H/SL(2,\mathbb{Z})$ is $\mathbb{C}(j)$.

If (E,C) is a complex elliptic curve together with a cyclic subgroup of order N, we can assume that $E = \mathbb{C}/\mathbb{Z} + \mathbb{Z}\tau$ and that the cyclic subgroup is generated by $\frac{\tau}{N}$. Then the isomorphism classes of such pairs correspond 1-1 to the points of the orbit space $H/\Gamma_0(N)$, where

$$\Gamma_0(N) = \{\, \begin{pmatrix} a & b \\ c & d \end{pmatrix} \in SL(2,\mathbb{Z}) : c \equiv 0\ (\mathrm{mod}\ N) \,\}.$$

For $N = 1$ we find again $H/SL(2,\mathbb{Z})$. The orbit space $H/\Gamma_0(N)$ is not compact. It can be compactified by adding a finite number of points. In fact, one can add in a natural way the orbits of $\mathbb{Q} \cup \{\infty\}/\Gamma_0(N)$. These orbits are called the cusps. For example, for $N = 1$ the set $\{z \in F : Im(z) > c > 1\}$ is mapped by $z \to \exp(2\pi iz)$ to a punctured disc $\{z \in \mathbb{C}^* : |z| < e^{-2\pi c}\}$. We now just add the origin of this disc. A local coordinate near this cusp is then $q = \exp(2\pi iz)$. By doing this for all cusps we thus obtain a projective algebraic curve (compact Riemann surface) $Y_0(N)$ over $\mathbb{C}$. We refer to [1] and [8] for more details.

The quotient E/C is again an elliptic curve. The function field of $X_0(N)$ is $\mathbb{Q}(j(E),j(E/C))$. Here $j(E)$ and $j(E/C)$ satisfy an algebraic relation, called the modular equation.

One can compute the genus of $X_0(N)$ over $\mathbf{F}_p$ (where p does not divide N) or over $\mathbb{C}$. It is the same for all these fields. Over $\mathbb{C}$ it can be computed using the Hurwitz-Zeuthen formula for the covering $Y_0(N) \to Y_0(1) = \mathbb{P}^1$. The result is (see [8]):

$$g(Y_0(N)) = 1 + \frac{1}{12}N\prod(1 + \frac{1}{p}) - \frac{a_2(N)}{4} - \frac{a_3(N)}{3} - \frac{1}{2}\Sigma_{d|n} \phi((d,\frac{N}{d})),$$

where ϕ is the Euler phi-function and

$a_2(N) = 0$ if 4 divides N,

$a_2(N) = \prod_{p|N} (1 + (\frac{-4}{p}))$ otherwise,

$a_3(N) = 0$ if N is even or 9 divides N,

$a_3(N) = \prod_{p|N}(1 + (\frac{-3}{p}))$ otherwise.

Here $(\frac{a}{p})$ is the Legendre symbol. For future use we note that if $N \to \infty$, then $g \to \infty$ and the dominant term in the formula for g is the second term.

4. Of course, we have to compute the number of points of $X_0(N)$ over $\mathbf{F}_{p^r}$. In fact we shall take $r=2$. The instrument to do this is the zeta function as we saw in lecture 4. Fortunately, in the case we consider, the zeta function can be described completely in terms of the curve $X_0(N)$ over $\mathbb{C}$.

We consider the space of regular differential forms on $Y_0(N)$ over $\mathbb{C}$. If ω is a regular differential form we restrict it to $X_0(N)$. It comes from a $\Gamma_0(N)$ -invariant differential form $f(z)dz$ on H under the quotient map $H \to X_0(N)$. Here $f(z)$ is a holomorphic function on H. We have

$$d(\frac{az+b}{cz+d}) = (cz + d)^{-2} dz,$$

so $f(z)dz$ is invariant under $\Gamma_0(N)$ if and only if

$$f(\frac{az+b}{cz+d}) = (cz + d)^2 f(z) \quad \text{for all } \left(\begin{smallmatrix} a & b \\ c & d \end{smallmatrix}\right) \text{ in } \Gamma_0(N). \tag{1}$$

Moreover, the expression $f(z)dz$ must extend over the cusps. A function satisfying these conditions is called a <u>cusp form of weight 2 on</u> $\Gamma_0(N)$. Conversely, every cusp form f of weight 2 on $\Gamma_0(N)$ defines a regular differential on $Y_0(N)$ via $f(z) \to f(z)dz$. The cusp forms of weight 2 on $\Gamma_0(N)$ form a vector space $S_2(\Gamma_0(N))$ of dimension g, where g is the genus of the complex curve $Y_0(N)$.

If $f \in S_2(\Gamma_0(N))$ then by (1) we have $f(z+1) = f(z)$, hence f admits a Fourier series

$$f = \Sigma_{n=1}^{\infty} b(n) q^n .$$

The fact that the series start with $n=1$ is due to the fact that the differential form $f(z)dz$ extends over the cusps.

On the vector space $S_2(\Gamma_0(N))$ there acts an algebra of operators, called the <u>Hecke operators</u>. The defintion is as follows. Let m be a positive integer prime to N. Consider the product of $X_0(N) \times X_0(N)$. Its points correspond to pairs of pairs (E,C). We consider in this product the correspondence (algebraic curve) $\Delta(m)$ consisting of all pairs $((E,C),(E',C'))$ with $E' = E/D$, $C' = $ image of C in E/D where D is a subgroup of E of order m. Over $\mathbb{C}$ we can describe this correspondence as follows. We consider in $H \times H$ all equations of the form

$$az_1z_2 + bz_1 + cz_2 + d = 0$$

where $(z_1,z_2) \in H \times H$ and $ad-bc = m$. They define a curve in $H/\Gamma_0(N) \times H/\Gamma_0(N)$. It extends to a correspondence on $Y_0(N) \times Y_0(N)$, again denoted by $\Delta(m)$. It is called the m-th Hecke correspondence. If ω is a regular differential form on $Y_0(N)$ we can pull it back to $\Delta(m)$ and push it forward to $Y_0(N)$. We find a differential form on $Y_0(N)$: we denote it by $T(m)^*\omega$. If ω comes from $f(z)dz$ on H and $T(m)^*\omega$ comes from $g(z)dz$ then we write: $T(m)f = g$. This defines an operator $T(m)$ on $S_2(\Gamma_0(N))$, called the <u>m-th Hecke operator</u>. One can compute its action on the Fourier expansion of f : the Hecke operator $T(m)$ with m a prime not dividing N acts on f by

$$f \rightarrow \sum_{n=1}^{\infty} b(n)q^{mn} + \sum_{n=1}^{\infty} b(mn)\, q^n.$$

We have for the operator $T(n)$ for n coprime to N :

$\qquad T(m)T(n) = T(ab)$ if $(m,n) = 1$,

$\qquad T(p^k) = T(p)T(p^{k-1}) - pT(p^{k-2})$ for a prime p with $(p,N) = 1$ and $k \geq 2$. (2)

One finds in this way a commutative algebra of operators acting on $S_2(\Gamma_0(N))$. On the vector space $S_2(\Gamma_0(N))$ there is a positive definite inner product, the <u>Petersson product</u> , defined by

$$<f,g> = \int f(z)g(z)\frac{dxdy}{y^2}.$$

The Hecke operators are hermitian with respect to this product :

$\qquad <T(m)f,g> = <f,T(m)g>.$

Therefore,we then can find a basis of common eigenforms for this whole algebra of operators, say $f_1, \dots ,f_g$. We write

$\qquad f_i = \sum_{n=1}^{\infty} b_i(n)\, q^n .$

One now observes that $b_i(1) \neq 0$ and we may then assume $b_i(1) = 1$. Indeed, we have $T(n)\, f_i = b_i(1)b_i(n)f_i$, so $b_i(1) = 0$ implies $f_i = 0$. We say that f_i is a <u>normalized eigenform</u> if $b_i(1) = 1$. We have

$T(r)f_i = b_i(r)\, f_i$ for every normalized eigenform in $S_2(\Gamma_0(N))$,

i.e. the Fourier coefficients of a normalized eigen form are its eigen values for the Hecke operators.

The basic fact is that the zeta function of $X_0(N)$ over $\mathbf{F}_p$ is expressible in terms of the Fourier coefficients $b_i(m)$ of these cusp forms f_i of weight 2. It is proved by computing the Hecke correspondence in characteristic p (Eichler-Shimura congruence relation).

(5.4) Theorem. The zeta function $Z(X_0(N),t)$ of $X_0(N)$ over $\mathbf{F}_p$ with p a prime not dividing N is of the form :

$$Z(X_0(N)/\mathbf{F}_p,t) = \frac{\prod_{i=1}^{g}(1-b_i(p)t+pt^2)}{(1-t)(1-pt)} .$$

5. Now we show that this theorem and a formula for the trace of $T(p^2)$ on $S_2(\Gamma_0(N))$ imply the desired result on codes if we assume that N is a prime. Indeed, from the formula for the zeta-function we have

$$\# X_0(N)(\mathbf{F}_p) = p+1- \textstyle\sum_{i=1}^{g} b_i(p)$$

$$\# X_0(N)(\mathbf{F}_{p^2}) = p^2+1 - \textstyle\sum_{i=1}^{g} b_i^2(p) + 2pg,$$

and if we use now that $b_i(p^2) = b_i^2(p) - p$ (a consequence of (2)), we see that

$$\# X_0(N)(\mathbf{F}_{p^2}) = p^2 + 1 - \textstyle\sum_{i=1}^{g} b_i(p^2) + gp .$$

But $\sum_{i=1}^{g} b_i(p^2)$ is the trace of the Hecke operator $T(p^2)$ on $S_2(\Gamma_0(N))$. Now the trace of the Hecke operators on $S_2(\Gamma_0(N))$ is known (see [2]):

$$\mathrm{Tr}\ T(p^2) = g + p^2 + 1 - \textstyle\sum\ (1+(\tfrac{D}{N}))\tfrac{h(D)}{w(D)} ,$$

where the sum is over all pairs (s,f) of integers s with $-2p < s < 2p$ and such that $D=(s^2-4p^2)/f^2$ is an integer $\equiv 0$ or 1 (mod 4).

If $N \to \infty$, then $g \to \infty$, and we find-- since g is the dominant term in $\mathrm{Tr}\ T(p^2)$ -- that

$$\# X_0(N)(\mathbf{F}_{p^2}) \approx g(p-1),$$

that is, we have (if we view $X_0(N)$ as a curve over $\mathbf{F}_{p^2}$, i.e. $N_1 = \# X_0(N)(\mathbf{F}_{p^2})$)

$$\frac{N_1}{g} \to p{-}1 = \sqrt{q} - 1.$$

(5.5) Theorem. (Tsfasman, Vladut, Zink [10]) There exists a sequence of Goppa codes over F_{p^2} such that $R + \delta$ has $1 - \frac{1}{p-1}$ as its limit.

Note that we know from Lecture 4 that $\lim \frac{N_1}{g} \leq p - 1$ (Drinfeld-Vladut). Therefore we find that $R + \delta$ has $1 - \frac{1}{p-1}$ as its limit and we cannot do better in this way.

(5.6) Corollary. There exist for $p \geq 7$ and $q = p^2$ limit points of Goppa codes in U_q lying above the Gilbert-Varshamov curve.
Proof. For $p \geq 7$ the line $R + \delta = 1 - \frac{1}{p-1}$ lies above the Gilbert-Varshamov curve for δ in a certain interval .   ◊

(5.7) Remark. In [10] this result was proved by exhibiting the points over F_{p^2} in a more explicit way. The points over F_{p^2} that we find correspond to supersingular elliptic curves. It is known that such curves are defined over F_{p^2}, see [9]. The approach using the trace formula can be found in a preprint of Moreno [7]. The theorem can be extended for all $q =$ even power of p. Recently, Zink has obtained also some results for $q = p^3$, see [11].

(5.8) Remark. The fact that the zeta function of $X_0(N)$ is known is due to the fact that the reduction modulo p of the Hecke correspondence $\Delta(p)$ can be computed by the so-called Eichler-Shimura congruence relation. It turns out that this reduction is the sum of two correspondences, the Frobenius correspondence and its transpose. This gives the relation with the α_i, the eigen values of Frobenius in cohomology.

References.

[1] Gunning,R.C.: Lectures on modular forms. Ann. of Math. Studies 48. Princeton Univ. Press 1962.
[2] Hijikata, : Explicit formula for the traces of the Hecke operators for $\Gamma_0(N)$. J. Math . Soc. Japan, 26,(1974), 56-80.

[3] Katz,N., Mazur,B.: Arithmetic moduli of elliptic curves. Ann. of Math. Studies Princeton Univ. Press. 1985.

[4] Lang, S.: Introduction to modular forms. Grundlehren 222. Springer Verlag.

[5] Manin, Yu. I. : What is the maximum number of points on a curve over F_2 ? J. Fac Sci. Univ. Tokyo. Sect. Ia Math. 28 (1981),715-720.

[6] Manin, Yu.I.,Vladut, S.G.: Linear codes and modular curves. Itogi Nauki i Techniki. Sovremennye Problemy Matematiki, tom 25 (1984).

[7] Moreno,C.: Goppa codes and modular curves. Preprint.

[8] Shimura,G.: Introduction to the arithmetic theory of automorphic forms. Publ. Math. Soc. Japan 11. Princeton Univ. Press, 1971.

[9] Silverman,J.H.: The arithmetic of elliptic curves. Grad. Texts in Math. 106. Springer Verlag 1985.

[10] Tsfasman, M.A.,Vladut,S.G., Zink, Th.: On Goppa codes which are better than the Varshamov-Gilbert bound. Math. Nachr. 109,(1982), 21-28.

[11] Zink,T.: Degeneration of Shimura surfaces and a problem in coding theory. Lecture Notes in Computer Science 199, 1986.

Index

affine variety	37
algebraic curve	40
alphabet	13
birational map	39
bitangent	59
canonical divisor (class)	48
canonical map	51
capacity	13
check polynomial	17
closed point	43
code	13
BCH	18
block	13
cyclic	17
dual	15
extended	16
generalized RS	20
Goppa	22
Hamming	16
irreducible cyclic	17
linear	15
MDS	19,26
optimal	4
primitive BCH	18
Reed-Solomon	19,20
self-dual	15,28
coordinate ring	37
coset leader	16
cusp form	77
degree of a divisor	43
differential form	47
dimension	40
distance	
Hamming	13
minimum	13
divisor	45
divisor class group	46
elliptic curve	53
entropy	15
equivalent	15
flex point	59
function field	37
generator matrix	49
genus	15
Gilbert-Varshamov curve	73

Goppa codes	55
Hecke operator	78
Hilbert Nullstellensatz	37
Hurwitz-Zeuthen	52
hyperelliptic curve	50
information rate	13
irreducible	37
linear equivalence	46
linear system	47
local ring	38
maximum likelihood	13
minimal polynomial	12
morphism	37
non-singular	40
parameter (local-)	41
parity check matrix	15
Plotkin bound	27
Plücker formula	51
ramification	52
rational differential form	47
rational function	39
rational map	39
regular differential form	47
regular function	38
residue	49
Riemann hypothesis	68
Riemann-Roch theorem	49
self-dual codes	63
Singleton bound	26
singular point	40
smooth	40
special	50
sphere packing bound	26
symbol error	13
syndrome decoding	15
trace	12
variety	37
weight	15
zeta function	66

Index of notations

Part I.

$\alpha(\delta)$	14
$A_q(n,d)$	14
$C^\perp$ – dual code	15
$\Gamma(L,g)$ – Goppa code	22
$d(\underline{x},\underline{y})$ – distance	13
$H_q(\delta)$ – entropy	25
$m_i(x)$ – minimal polynomial	12
$[n,k]$ code	15
(n,M,d) code	14
$Tr(\xi)$ – trace	12
$V_q(n,d)$	25
$<\underline{x},\underline{y}>$	15

Part II.

a_r – modified number of points	68
α_i – roots	67
$A(q)$ – $\limsup N_1/g$	69
$\beta_q(\delta)$ – entropy function	73
$C(D,G), C^*(D,G)$ – Goppa codes	55
δ – min. Distance/length	57
$|D|$ – linear system	47
F_q – finite field with q elements	43
g_d^r – linear system	50
$\Gamma_0(N)$ – modular group	76
j – classical j-function	74

K – canonical divisor (class)	48
$k[X]$ – coordinate ring	37
$k(X)$ – function field	39
k_v – residue field	43
$L(D)$ – vector space of rational functions	46
N_r – number of points over field with q^r elements	67
$N_q(g)$ – max. number of points on genus g curve over F_q	70
P_i – characteristic polynomial	67
$O(U)$ – ring of regular functions	38
O_x – local ring	38
$Pic(X)$ – group of divisor classes	53
R – information rate	57
res – residue	49
$S_2(\Gamma_0(N))$ – space of cusp forms of weight 2	77
$T(m)$ – Hecke operator	78
U_q – domain of codes	73
$X_0(N)$ – modular curve	75
$Z(X,t)$ – zeta function	66
$\zeta(X,s)$ – zeta function	66
$\Omega(E)$ – space of differentials	55
$\Omega[X]$ – module of regular differentials	47
$[n,k,d]$ – linear code with parameters n,k,d	59

DMV SEMINAR

Edited by the German Mathematics Society

Vol. 1
Manfred Knebusch/
Winfried Scharlau
Algebraic Theory of
Quadratic Forms
Generic Methods and Pfister Forms
1980. 48 pages, Softcover
ISBN 3-7643-1206-8

Vol. 2
Klas Diederich/Ingo Lieb
Konvexität in der komplexen
Analysis
Neue Ergebnisse und Methoden
1981. 150 Seiten, Broschur
ISBN 3-7643-1207-6

Vol. 3
S. Kobayashi/H. Wu with the
collaboration of C. Horst
Complex Differential Geometry
Topics in Complex Differential
Geometry. Function Theory on
Non-compact Kähler Manifolds
2nd edition 1987.
160 pages, Softcover
ISBN 3-7643-1494-X

Vol. 4
R. Lazarsfeld/ A. Van de Ven
Topics in the Geometry of
Projective Space
Recent Work of F.L. Zak
1984. 52 pages, Softcover
ISBN 3-7643-1660-8

Vol. 5
Wolfgang Schmidt
Analytische Methoden für
Diophantische Gleichungen
Einführende Vorlesungen
1984. 132 Seiten, Broschur
ISBN 3-7643-1661-6

Vol. 6
A. Delgado/D. Goldschmidt/
B. Stellmacher
Groups and Graphs:
New Results and Methods
1985. 244 pages, Softcover
ISBN 3-7643-1736-1

Vol. 7
R. Hardt/L. Simon
Seminar on Geometric
Measure Theory
1986. 118 pages, Softcover
ISBN 3-7643-1815-5

Vol. 8
Yum-Tong Siu
Lectures on Hermitian-Einstein
Metrics for Stable Bundles and
Kähler-Einstein Metrics
1987. 172 pages, Softcover
ISBN 3-7643-1931-3

Vol. 9
Peter Gaenssler/Winfried Stute
Seminar on Empirical Processes
1987. 114 pages, Softcover
ISBN 3-7643-1921-6

Vol. 10
Jürgen Jost
Nonlinear Methods in Riemannian
and Kählerian Geometry
Delivered at the German Mathe-
matical Society Seminar in
Düsseldorf, June 1986
1988. 154 pages, Softcover
ISBN 3-7643-1920-8

Vol. 11
Tammo tom Dieck/Ian Hambleton
Surgery Theory and Geometry of
Representations
1988. 122 pages, Softcover
ISBN 3-7643-2204-7

Birkhäuser
Verlag AG
Basel · Boston · Berlin